Convers
Activism

Conversations About Activism and Change

Independent Living Movement Ireland
and Thirty Years of Disability Rights

Edited by
Sarah Fitzgerald

MARTELLO

CONVERSATIONS ABOUT ACTIVISM AND CHANGE
First published in 2023 by
Martello Publishing
Glenshesk House
10 Richview Office Park
Clonskeagh
Dublin D14 V8C4
Republic of Ireland
martellopublishing.ie

Paperback ISBN: 978-1-7396086-0-6
eBook ISBN: 978-1-7396086-1-3

A CIP record for this title is available from the British Library.

Typeset by JVR Creative India
Cover design and typesetting by Alan Keogh
Photography by John Owens
Printed by SprintPrint, Dublin

Declan O'Keefe was a founding member of ILMI who sadly passed away on Thursday, 3 October 2019 after a short illness. Declan generously left a bequest to ILMI, and to honour Declan's contribution as a founding member ILMI are proud to use his bequest to bring this book to life.

Declan was a librarian and keen patron of the arts. We hope that Declan's generosity will inspire the future leaders of the disability rights movement in Ireland to follow in the footsteps of these and so many other brilliant activists, including those who are no longer with us, in coming together to form a strong collective of disabled people.

Contents

Introduction

Damien Walshe
CEO, Independent Living Movement Ireland

Thirty years ago, seven disabled people began a journey that fundamentally changed Irish society when they embarked on setting up the very first Personal Assistance Service (PAS) in Ireland and established the Centre for Independent Living (CIL), which later became Independent Living Movement Ireland (ILMI).

They wanted what non-disabled people took for granted: to make their own choices in where they lived and who they lived with, when they got up, what they wanted to wear and to eat, where they wanted to go and what they wanted to do with their lives. They wanted the freedom to choose and they began the journey of independent living in Ireland. Their legacy lives on within the movement today, although that legacy is as yet to be fully realised.

The journey for disabled people's equality in Ireland pre-dates the formation of ILMI and much has been achieved by disabled people in making Ireland more inclusive. However, much of that memory hasn't been documented or recorded and many of the projects, campaigns and actions led by disabled people are often unknown by younger disabled people looking to further advance their rights. This book is part of reclaiming that "hidden history" about the struggle for the liberation and self-determination of disabled people in Ireland.

During the Covid-19 pandemic, ILMI expanded our video conferencing to connect disabled people on a cross-impairment basis, responding creatively to the crisis to create numerous online spaces to bring disabled people together. The pandemic "forced" us all online and in doing so broke down geographical and physical barriers for disabled people. Online engagement is accessible to most: it removes the challenge of inaccessible transport and the lack of PAS hours. Connecting virtually by Zoom brought an opportunity to find new ways of bringing disabled people together through online gatherings.

A real sense of community and connection was created in our meetings, which not only focused on policy and campaigns, but peer support and a real willingness to create social gatherings. One of our earliest social spaces was an ILMI Film Club created and curated by one of our staff members, Dr James Casey: the Oscar-nominated Netflix film *Crip Camp* had just been released and James facilitated a lively discussion among ILMI members.

One of the things James noticed was that there was an understandable gap in knowledge in relation to disability rights struggles in Ireland between younger and older activists. Many of the more established activists shared stories of comrades who had passed and campaigns lost and won. All the younger activists had gone through mainstream education, benefitting from campaigns for inclusive education, but until they connected with ILMI they lacked a space to connect with other disabled people. Not surprisingly most of the younger activists knew nothing about struggles in the past but were eager to learn. From the early ILMI Film Club conversations it was clear that for our movement to build an inclusive Ireland it was going to have to generate ways to capture that history.

This chimed in with discussions that Des Kenny and Sarah Fitzgerald were already having about how the movement needed to begin to capture its own narrative to ensure that the legacy of the collective work of disabled people was archived in some way. From this, a series of online interviews were held with twelve disabled activists. After each discussion there was a chance for questions and answers about past campaigns, fallen comrades and the need to continue to share our collective histories. The overwhelming feeling from those who listened in "live" was that the stories captured need to be kept as some form of record so that disabled people (and non-disabled people) could learn about disability equality in Ireland.

Those conversations were made into podcasts and it was at this stage that Sarah Fitzgerald saw the opportunity to edit those conversations and create a tangible resource that would begin to document a part of the disability rights movement in Ireland.

As Sarah began that monumental task, ILMI received a bequest from the passing of one of our seven founding members, the late Declan O'Keefe. Declan was a keen patron of the arts and the board of ILMI felt that a fitting tribute to Declan's memory was to use some of that bequest to turn those late-night conversations about activism and change into a book that could spark the light in the next generation of disabled activists.

The result of that process – from an online discussion about a Netflix film – is this book. Those conversations about activism and change were a way of capturing that hidden history and connecting some of the disabled activists involved in campaigning for change with a wider audience of disabled and non-disabled people.

As a cross-impairment national Disabled Persons Organisation (DPO), ILMI's vision is an Ireland where disabled persons have freedom, choice and control over all aspects of their lives and can fully participate in an inclusive society as equals. Central to achieving that inclusion is building a shared understanding of what we mean when we talk about disability. Throughout this book you will hear the importance of the social model of disability and how it informs and connects the activists in these pages.

The social model looks at how society is structured and how it disables people. It isn't based on a person's impairment; it is about what barriers exist in terms of attitudes, policy development, access or lack of supports that prevent people from participating in society as equals, with choice and control over their own lives. In this model it is society that disables people from achieving their hopes and dreams – not a person's impairment.

The social model informs all aspects of the work of ILMI. As a campaigning, national representative organisation that promotes the philosophy of independent living we are working to build an inclusive society. Central to the way we work is to ensure that policy decisions that have an impact on the lives of disabled people must be directly influenced by those whose lives are directly affected.

ILMI's work is to develop policies and campaigns based on disabled people's lived experiences in order to remove barriers that restrict life choices for disabled people. When barriers are removed, disabled people can be independent and equal in society, with choice and control over their own lives. Barriers are not just physical. Attitudes found in society, based on prejudice or stereotypes (also called ableism), also disable people from having equal opportunities to be part of society. Disabled people developed the social model of disability because the traditional medical model did not explain their personal experience of disability or help to develop more inclusive ways of living.

The social model of disability informs key international conventions such as the UN Convention of the Rights of People with Disabilities (UNCRPD) and is in contrast to the "medical/charity model" of disability. The medical/charity model individualises disability and promotes the idea that people are disabled by their impairments or differences. The medical model always focuses on people's impairments from a medical perspective. In some ways it still looks at what is "wrong" with the person and not what the person needs. It creates low expectations and leads to people losing independence, choice and control in their own lives. The medical/charity model never recognises the rights of disabled people and assumes that disabled people need to be "looked after" or "cared for". The medical/charity model has professionals make decisions for disabled people.

In beginning a conversation about activism and change with the reader, we hope that each of the personal narratives contributes to a greater understanding of the social model of disability so that disabled people and their allies can work to remove the structural barriers that continue to prevent the full and active participation of disabled people in Irish society.

The publication of this book coincides with thirty years of independent living in Ireland and there has been significant progress through campaigns led by disabled people, which this book outlines. But that is not the end of this journey: it is only the beginning. Having ratified the UNCRPD in 2018, Ireland is now committed to progressively realising the rights of disabled people to participate in society as equals. This means moving away from outdated systems that segregate disabled people and limit their choices and expectations. It means moving towards *only* investing in supports that give disabled people choice and control and build inclusion.

The aim of this book is not only to inspire disabled people to continue to work collectively to struggle to have their right to participate in society as equals, but also to encourage non-disabled people to hear the voices of disabled people.

We hope that non-disabled allies who are reading this book recognise that for a truly inclusive society we need to ensure that disabled people's voices are always heard. As a society we need to continually ask ourselves: what is the State doing to give disabled people the supports they need to fully participate in society and fulfil their potential?

Conversations About Activism and Change gives us a real insight into the impact disabled people have had in creating change in Ireland over the last thirty years, but also sets out the changes that still need to be brought about. Hopefully these conversations will spark that change now and into the future.

Foreword

Niall Crowley

Conversations about activism and change are important in a context where activism is not as widespread as it needs to be. They are vital in a context where change is not as quick as it needs to be. Conversations about activism and change, which enable activists to tell their story about their journey to becoming activists and their experience of being activists, are all too rare. They need to be celebrated for stimulating a sustained tradition and enabling a critical mass of activism.

The conversations in this publication confirm the truth of current activists having a key contribution to make in enabling new activists to emerge. They highlight the role played by other activists in sparking and enabling new activists on their journey towards activism. In telling their story, the narrators thus repay a debt to those that drew them into the search for social change, those that mentored their early activism. The narrators offer a history to a new generation of activists; a history that encourages and informs this new generation in rising to the challenge of realising a more equal society.

Activism is not widely encouraged in our society. It is tamed by powerholders that deem it to be trouble-making. It is limited for lack of resources and supports made available. It is snagged in bureaucracy, false starts and endless meetings and submissions. Yet, as we know from the stories told, that activism makes a difference. It is clear that a more equal society will only be realised by sustained and widespread activism.

Activism is not easy. The stories tell of tense meetings, the need for clarity among activists and the challenge for activists to ask questions of themselves. Setbacks are noted as draining energy and involvement. Activism fatigue can set in, making it hard to keep going. Activism takes an emotional toll. The stories highlight the importance of creating spaces for peer support, safe spaces for activists to mind each other and spaces for reflection and learning to be an effective activist.

The inequalities that continue to distort our society are such that there can be no argument as to the need for change. Change, however, does not come easily or quickly here, in particular change for equality. The stories are clear that, despite some achievements, many issues still need to be addressed and progress is painfully slow. This reality underpins the importance of activism and the imperative of sustaining, growing and evolving activism to achieve change that is characterised by greater speed and ambition.

The stories told are of individual activism, but they are all clear as to the centrality of the collective, and the need for movement-building if an impact is to be made. Progressing change involves a shift from "I" to "We". Movement-building is about assembling the power to challenge inequality more effectively and to advance the demand for social change with greater force and impact. Threaded through the stories are approaches and initiatives taken, which add up to give us a picture of what is required for effective movement-building.

Movement-building requires a vision for change, behind which people and organisations can mobilise and be mobilised. It involves organising people and building organisations to advance the demand for this change. It needs collaboration, solidarity and co-ordination across different sectors of society that share issues and goals. It involves creativity in the actions taken to put forward the demand for change. These are the key elements that underpin the power required for a movement to make an impact.

Activism is too often focused on what we don't want, challenging and decrying the problems faced. There is clarity and a sense of urgency in the stories about the barriers disabled people face in seeking equality: barriers of internalised oppression, of excluding practice, of culture and attitudes riddled with stereotypes, and of key systems that disadvantage. These barriers have to be challenged and removed, but these stories usefully emphasise the need to be solution-focused in doing so. Activism must promote what we want, the nature of the more equal society we desire if it is to mobilise people behind the social change needed.

This is where the power of ideas comes into play, the ability of the activist to imagine what a more equal society looks like and how it might best be organised. The stories emphasise the social model of disability, and the work done in developing and promoting this analysis, as the key starting point for such a vision. Equality, the stories tell us, involves a society characterised by independence, choice, autonomy, freedom, control, participation, inclusion and social justice. Concretising this understanding of a more equal society, in specific demands for the social change we want, emerges as key to movement-building.

Strong organisations and their establishment, rooted in the common ground of shared identity and experience among those involved, is another form of power that is emphasised in the stories. Disabled people's organisations (DPOs) create a sense of solidarity and build the collective that is central to advancing change. The stories celebrate the emergence of an abundance of DPOs while emphasising the need to overcome fragmentation and forge alliances between them. Effectiveness requires an organising of organisations.

Effectiveness further requires the organising of people. The stories emphasise the grass-roots work of organising needed, the knocking on doors to engage and mobilise people, and the provision of learning opportunities to ensure the emergence of a coherent and informed collective. Such opportunities encompass learning about how the system works, how to work together, the nature of injustice and inequality and how change happens.

The stories tell of the need for allies of non-disabled people to be involved in demanding equality for disabled people. This perspective goes further in challenging DPOs to take a broader focus and get involved in other human rights movements. Collaboration of this nature, rooted in solidarity and enabling co-ordination, breaks down the silos that divide those various forces and groups seeking an equal society. Collaboration between movements is essential in creating an empowered demand for change.

Collaboration is underpinned by the intersectionality in the stories. Disability is deemed to be one part of one's identity, alongside such as class, gender or ethnicity and beyond. This intersectionality is the common ground on which collaboration is forged. The shared demand for an equal society is empowered where all groups experiencing inequality and their movements work together for a shared vision of and effective demand for an equal society.

Creativity, the capacity to surprise jaded perspectives and to disrupt the way things normally run, is a vital ingredient of the effective movement. Tactics need thoughtful consideration and design. Effective tactics require imagination. A broad repertoire of tactics is needed for impact but is rarely in evidence. The stories, however, point to a valuable and creative diversity in the tactics employed by the narrators.

The tactics identified encompass but are not limited to an engagement with the personnel, structures and systems of the state and relevant institutions. They further include protest actions and campaigns. They involve cultural action using theatre, stories and song, where the artist and activist combine. Litigation and use of the courts is pursued. The tactics deployed make good use of external levers available such as EU-level and UN-level developments, most notably the UNCRPD.

These conversations about activism and change start by looking back at the history that holds the foundations for current and future activism. We need to know this history from the perspective of those who lived it, for the confidence it offers that change is possible and for the bedrock it provides for new ambition and new forms of activism and movement-building.

The challenge to plan strategically for the future is noted in the stories. The past will tell us where we have come from and how we got here; the future will tell us where we need to go to and how to get there. The next generation of activists are challenged to hear and understand this history, just as they are challenged to look to that future and to define and establish how best to realise that future. Conversations about activism and change must continue, therefore, in deliberating on this future. The stories told importantly note that the platforms for such conversations are already in place.

Niall Crowley is author of Civil Society for Equality and Environmental Sustainability: Re-imagining a Force for Change, *published by TASC and St Stephen's Green Trust in 2022.*

Preface

Sarah Fitzgerald

Disabled people are all too familiar with fighting to be included in society, but we also know that we do not face these battles in isolation. We all know that real social change can only be brought about if we work together as a collective. But when we scratch beneath the surface, what does that mean? What are the ingredients of a strong disability movement?

Conversations about Activism and Change offers a collection of personal insights into the development of the Independent Living Movement in Ireland. Too often the lives and experiences of disabled people are portrayed by those deemed qualified to speak on their behalf. However, it is worth remembering that here in Ireland we are masters of storytelling, and for generations, stories and folklore have been passed down from our elders. *Conversations* captures the voices of disabled activists themselves, and through their stories the triumphs and learning achieved through building the Irish disability movement come to the fore. Not only are these stories snapshots of the past, they can also provide a roadmap for disabled activists seeking guidance in continuing their activism journey into the future.

Eleven activists, with different backgrounds and experiences, were asked to consider their role in building a disability movement. Although each story in this collection can be read as a stand-alone piece, there are a couple of common threads that can be pulled together, creating a people's history of the Independent Living Movement in Ireland.

The most important message that comes through in reading these stories is that in order to form a strong collective, it is vital for disabled people as individuals to challenge their internalised oppression and recognise that it is the physical, attitudinal and organisational barriers, not our impairments, that exclude us from society. Internalised oppression is a by-product of the medical-model approach to disability. Some activists in this collection, including Jacqui Browne and Maureen

McGovern, recall spending much of their childhood in institutions and hospital settings, and Maureen admits that the experience left her "institutionalised in many ways". Ann Marie Flanagan recalls the mixed feelings of freedom and guilt when she used an electric wheelchair for the first time, feeling that using it was somehow letting her parents down: "I believed that using an electric wheelchair would be a backwards step... but I remember the feelings of equality and autonomy with someone walking beside me for the first time – it was surreal."

However, segregation in the form of residential settings and special education is not always necessarily a negative experience, and while Des Kenny recalls a sense of sadness in being separated from his family, Peter Kearns and Eileen Daly highlight how their experience of "the special school system" enabled them to forge alliances with their disabled peers and to build a sense of solidarity.

Embracing the social model of disability has been described as a 'road to Damascus' experience by many of our storytellers, including Selina Bonnie. Selina says that her lightbulb moment happened when she met the late Martin Naughton for the first time:

Out of nowhere, this man in a hat I'd never met before flew into the room in his powerchair. There was this sense that the king had arrived. Even the highest-ranking politician seemed to respect him. I remember thinking, *Who is that?* It was Martin Naughton. Never before had I seen somebody in a wheelchair command so much power.

Locating the barriers or "problems" outside of disabled people themselves is the first step in bringing about change. Peter Kearns believes that living in accordance with the principles of the social model is key in building a disability movement: "I think that once we recognise that it's the various barriers that disable us, then we share common ground. For me, an impairment is an individual experience, whereas embracing the social model allows us to build a collective."

Eileen Daly would be quick to point out, however, that the disability movement in Ireland wasn't strictly business only. Many strong friendships were forged, which enabled these activists and others to feel comfortable in coming together as a collective. These people learned together, made many mistakes and laughed and cried about their triumphs and defeats. They helped each other and, in turn, reached out to educate their peers and show them that they, too, were entitled to have their human rights met. They recalled how these friendships changed their lives, including the friendship of those who have since passed away.

Throughout these stories, important milestones in the history of the Independent Living Movement are mentioned: the establishment of local Centres for Independent Living (CIL), including the first Irish CIL, in Dublin in 1992; the 1996 Report from the Commission of the Status of People with Disabilities and, most recently in March 2017, the ratification of the UNCRPD. These are significant achievements that could only be brought about through disabled people themselves working in solidarity.

One particular event that stood out in the minds of many of these activists were the leader-organised and -led "actions" in 2012 (Martin Naughton never used the word "protests", according to Selina) against blanket cuts to the Personal Assistance Service. James Reilly, the then Minister for Health, had threatened cuts of €12 million, which would effectively eradicate the Personal Assistance Service in Ireland, relegating many disabled people to nursing homes and leaving them unable to work or contribute to society. These leaders saved thousands of disabled people in Ireland from losing their Personal Assistance Service.

However, in congratulating ourselves on our past achievements, it is vital to look to the future of the Independent Living Movement and to come together once again to face challenges head-on. Des Kenny likens the movement to an orchestra, "comprising different musicians playing different disability instruments. We all play our part in achieving harmony and tunefulness." There is also a consensus that to progress as a movement we need to be open and willing to work with allies who can help us bring about social change. Jacqui Browne observed that "[to keep the] movement going, we need to identify 'champions', not only within our movement but outside of that movement as well. If we get caught up in a 'nothing about us without us' approach, we will lose out as a movement." It seems that one of the true benchmarks of a strong disability collective is having the good sense to recognise that we cannot do this on our own and that we will only achieve true equality when we enlist others outside of the movement into our cause.

After all, one of the cornerstones of the Independent Living Movement is that as disabled people we do not work alone or in isolation. As long as we are facilitated in using our own voices and telling our own stories, there is no limit to the greatness that we as a movement can achieve.

I would like to thank Damien Walshe and Des Kenny for affording me this opportunity to explore this people's history of the Independent Living Movement. It is my deepest hope that those who read these stories are reinvigorated by them, and that they always remember that even during the toughest challenges, as long as we work together, we are never alone.

Sarah Fitzgerald
November 2022

Des Kenny

I was fortunate enough to have enjoyed a full working life prior to my retirement, which is no mean achievement given that my educational journey began in a "special school" – St Joseph's School for the Blind – in Dublin. I had to travel to Dublin from Newbridge in County Kildare. Although Newbridge is only a short distance from Dublin, the journey took nearly two hours in the late fifties and early sixties. There was no local integrated education at the time.

I will never forget how sad I felt to be separated from my family. I was the eldest of what would grow to be a family of nine children. My poor father, having given up on a cure from doctors and hospitals for a serious injury to one eye and complications with the other eye, took me on a number of occasions to a nearby holy well that had a reputation in folklore for miraculous cures. But again my father was disappointed that we found no cure for my eyesight, which was now developing into blindness.

My education was made more challenging by the lack of Braille books and facilities. Although I studied to the best of my ability and left school with the equivalent in some subjects of a Leaving Cert, I did not receive the official State certificate. It would be a further two years after I had left school before the Department of Education would set the official Leaving Certificate for blind and vision-impaired students.

I was conscious of the deficits in my education (an awareness most of us felt on leaving special school). I started attending classes in the Dublin Institute of Adult Education, where I obtained a diploma in social studies. Here I also took classes in public speaking, leading to me becoming auditor of the Institute's debating society. It was at this time that my social consciousness was awakened and I started my journey into activism by taking small steps. My inaugural debate as auditor was titled Community Responsibility for the Disadvantaged. Surprisingly, I was terrified of speaking in public until I became involved with the debating society and grew in confidence.

As an adult evening student, in the early seventies I set out to do an arts degree at UCD, but the study materials were not accessible to me, and it was impractical to constantly ask others to read for me. With some disappointment, I abandoned my studies after the end of the first year. Later I went back to education and obtained an MSc (Econ) in health-care management from Newport College in Wales and an MBA via The Open University.

My first job after leaving school was as a Braille transcriber for the Irish Association for the Blind (IAB) in 1966, which was later subsumed into the National Council for the Blind of Ireland (NCBI) in 1988. The organisation had a Braille and audio library where materials were transcribed into Braille and recorded as audio as well. I stayed there for eight years, before moving to the National League of the Blind of Ireland (NLBI) for six years. From there I took a major leap into activism as a trade union official. The NLBI was a specialist trade union that protected the terms and conditions of employment of the seventy workers in the sheltered workshops for the blind at Rathmines, in Dublin, and supported the employment of over 150 blind telephonists in the public service and local authorities. The Irish

Association for the Blind and the National League of the Blind were both disabled persons' organisations (DPOs) run by boards made up of people who were blind or had low vision.

I was learning how to lobby for and bring about change by moseying my way into the company of influencers. These influencers included the late Liam Maguire, who was involved in the formative days of the Irish Wheelchair Association (IWA) and Disabled Peoples' International (DPI). Liam and I were appointed at the same time to the board of the National Rehabilitation Board (NRB), where we established a good working relationship with Dr Joe Robins, an influential assistant secretary in the Department of Health at that time. Liam Maguire was one of the first powerfully motivated disabled people I had come across. Before his motorcycle accident, he had already achieved stature for himself as an activist with the Workers' Union of Ireland and in his employment as a shop steward at Dublin Airport, a role he returned to after his rehabilitation at the National Rehabilitation Hospital. Liam brought back stories of the fledgling disability movement through his membership of DPI. I started to also look abroad at the approaches taken in other countries, particularly Scandinavia. We became interested in what was happening outside of Ireland and how work done in other countries might be "translated" for an Irish context. We didn't always agree on the same approaches to change, but our different ways of thinking and doing were complementary in achieving changes in the employment placement services of the NRB, and sheltered workshops. The aim was to address the prevalence of using disabled people as a form of cheap labour, as was later highlighted in Christian O'Reilly's play, *Sanctuary*. It was also a campaign to move job-seeking for disabled people out of the health sector to the Department of Labour.

Through my involvement with the NRB, I interacted with people who had started some of the newer voluntary organisations at that time: John Bermingham (Cope Foundation), Valerie Goulding (Central Remedial Clinic), Dr Barbara Stokes (St Michael's House) and Frank Cahill (Rehab). I also became an admirer of Brian Malone and Colm O'Doherty's campaigning on behalf of wheelchair users. It was during this time that I became conscious of the tension between people with congenital impairments and those with acquired impairments, a tension that exists to this day.

In 1980 I began a stint of six years as CEO of the Disability Federation of Ireland (DFI) under its old name of the Union of Voluntary Organisations for the Handicapped (UVOH). This was a challenging time to be involved in managing the relationship between the voluntary bodies and the health boards, before the shift towards the industrialisation of disability into the "voluntary sector". In 1986 I became the CEO of the National Council for the Blind of Ireland (NCBI), a post from which I retired in 2013. Now I use the free time my retirement has afforded me as an opportunity to write poetry.

As for the process of influencing change, and the slow rate at which change is created, I would remind people of what US activist Judy Heumann says in her autobiography *Being Heumann*: "The process of democracy is slow." To be an effective advocate, one needs to be comfortable in one's own skin. I believe that such confidence stems from mixing with others and sharing experiences across life and society rather than necessarily being related only to disability itself.

In the 1990s I was fortunate to experience the beginnings of some far-reaching changes at the European level, for example the introduction of Braille on pharmaceutical packaging, as well as on lift control panels. I was able to influence the installation of audio signals at pedestrian crossings in Dublin in the late 1970s, and we had to again highlight the importance of this measure to traffic officials in the City Council some thirty years later when there was an attempt to unfairly turn off some of them. Progress continues to be made, nonetheless – audio alert devices have been included in all new electric vehicles since January 2021.

I believe in the power of the collective. If I may compare the disability movement to an orchestra comprising different musicians playing different disability instruments, we all play our part in achieving harmony and tunefulness. I also believe that the ratification of the UNCRPD has the potential to unlock true equality for disabled people in Ireland. I would describe it as a score to which we need to work out the beat and arrangement.

There is a danger that in having won some rights, we are regressing from an equality perspective. I believe that, as a collective, we need to form a DPO that represents people of all levels and types of impairment. Recognising the diversity within Ireland's disability movement, I would favour the creation within a DPO of subgroups or "rooms" to discuss and address issues specific to different types of disabilities. That said, we must be able to bring that diversity together and work in a unified fashion as a truly representative DPO.

I joined the board of Independent Living Movement Ireland (ILMI) in 2019 and am currently serving as chairperson. In keeping with the mission statement of the organisation, I am particularly anxious that Article 19 of the UNCRPD is implemented in Ireland. Article 19 outlines the right of people with disabilities to independent living, should this be what they aspire to. I believe that the realisation of Article 19 depends on a number of factors, including having links with the community, having accessible transport and infrastructure and adequate access to the Personal Assistance Service for those who need it most. People don't want to be locked up in nursing homes or places of care. It begs the question, however: to achieve this, are we prepared to crawl up the steps of the plinth at the Dáil like the early campaigners of the disability movement in the US crawled up the steps of their legislature?

As a caution I would remind people of activism fatigue. It lurks in the background and it can have a negative effect on the progression of any civil rights movement. To avert this negative tendency, I would suggest we seek out and enlist the assistance of people and groups who are willing to work with disabled people as our allies.

Eileen Daly

My journey began when I went to my local primary
school at the age of five. I was the only wheelchair user,
and over time I began to feel a little excluded. It was
an all-girls school, which didn't help. At the age of ten,
I chose to attend a special school. I was just tired of
standing out, and it turned out to be one of the best
decisions I've ever made. It shaped the person I am
today, and one teacher in particular really motivated
and challenged me, so it was a positive experience. I
made lots of friends and it was the beginning of my
journey into activism. I followed the standard curricu-
lum and progressed to secondary school. Thankfully I
never fell into the trap of having to lower my expectations of myself, as can sometimes happen within
"special" educational environments. Another advantage
was that I was able to access services such as physio-
therapy. Sadly, when I entered mainstream education, I

couldn't keep these appointments and I had no time to do the exercises, which meant that some of my physical abilities deteriorated. It struck me that there were some inequalities, even within the bubble of special education, between those who were more able and those who had significant impairments. I now feel that if my peers had maybe been challenged a little more, perhaps they might've had a different future ahead of them.

I decided that I needed to move back to a mainstream school as I had ambitions, including going to college and getting a job. I would describe my secondary school experience as challenging. I attended a mainstream secondary school and was expected to compete with my fellow students despite the absence of reasonable accommodations. I did my Junior Cert without any accommodations or scribes, but still managed to get Bs and Cs. I remember in particular sitting the compulsory SATs in third year. The purpose of the SATs was to help identify a student's stronger subjects and determine their career path. Without accommodations, my impairment put me at an immediate disadvantage as I couldn't manage to do the exams within the allocated timeframe. At that time there were no special needs assistants (SNAs). It was an awful experience. I had a heated exchange with the principal and I told her that I wasn't deformed. My SAT test results were not good and I was devastated. However, it also marked an important moment: I decided that I wanted to be a guidance counsellor and to help others. I wanted to help create a more flexible system. I was granted a scribe for my Leaving Cert and that was a much more positive experience.

The access officer told me that I wouldn't get enough points to study in college and that I should consider a PLC instead. I was nonetheless determined to go to college. A representative from the National Rehabilitation Board (NRB) came to my home to have a "chat" with me about my future and suggested that I apply for work in Jacob's biscuit factory. I told my mother that there was no way I was going to a day centre, and she supported me on this. A month later, *In from the Margins* – a TV documentary that followed how disabled people lived during the early nineties – was aired. It featured Donal Toolan, Joe T. Mooney, Martin Naughton and Ursula Hegarty, and they all spoke about the emergence of the Independent Living Movement. I decided that I wanted to live independently and go to college. I made contact with Martin and the Centre for Independent

Living (CIL) after my place at UCD was confirmed, and we worked on getting a package together. After being refused by the Health Board and the National Rehabilitation Board, I told them that I was going to bring it to the European Court of Human Rights!

I put arts in UCC as my first choice on the CAO form. I went to visit UCC and it wasn't as progressive as it is now. It was my mother who encouraged me to fill out the change-of-mind form and apply for UCD. In 1994 I decided to do a three-year degree in UCD in social science, and I started speaking up, promoting inclusion for disabled students. Like many students I studied hard and partied harder. After graduating, I didn't particularly want to work in the disability sector, but after being unemployed for a year, I started my first job with the Irish Wheelchair Association on a Community Employment scheme. It was around this time that my passion for equal rights came to the fore. Martin Naughton became a huge influence in my life. He was the one who opened doors at a time when people were trying to close them, and I feel that he is the reason I am where I am now. From there, I became involved with CIL, where I felt included and accepted. Everyone was so welcoming, and I felt I just naturally fit in. During this time I met other allies, including Florence Dougall, Joe T. Mooney, Eugene Callan and John Doyle, all of whom I counted not just as allies but as close friends. It wasn't all about activism – it was also about companionship, swapping stories about our love lives and having fun. That social aspect was so important, and it still is.

I remember well the protests of 2012, which were held in response to a decision taken by the Minister for Health at the time, James Reilly, to make savage cutbacks to the Personal Assistance budget. I wasn't directly involved, unfortunately, as I was recovering from surgery at the time. It was one of the first times that we as disabled people were seen as a force to be reckoned with. We came together as a collective and the result was very powerful. It led to the realisation that we cannot work in isolation. We need to plan strategically and ensure that rights are always on the agenda. Crucially, people with impairments need a safe space to air their views and to know their views will be respected, even if those views are different from others'.

I was appointed to the National Council for Special Education in March 2019 by the National Disability Authority. I took my appointment seriously and didn't want to be seen as coming in with my own agenda. I feel that my lived experience and my ability to relate to others really help me in my role. Progress is slow, but I hope that I make a difference. I have always been open with my colleagues about my identity as an activist and I have been able to put the principles of inclusion and equality into practice. I also relish the opportunity to learn from other professionals across different fields. I take the responsibility of representing my peers seriously, and I believe in not only ensuring access for those with physical disabilities but also in taking a cross-impairment approach. It's important that disabled people are at the table in bringing about change.

I feel fortunate insofar as I can use my workspace to collaborate with schools, SNAs, parents, teachers and of course disabled students themselves in addressing the barriers that exclude them from society. I can also bring my activism into my work, and I've been told that my personal lived experience is an asset in my role. I feel that my ability to relate to people on many different levels is a huge advantage.

As a more experienced activist, I would love to see the movement take a more cross-impairment approach. We need to work with each other and challenge each other. I would really love to see younger disabled people using their voice. Ideally all young people should be learning about rights and equality from an early age. Some people don't realise that they have a right to their own opinions, but you can't force people to use their voices, either. The world is evolving and the coronavirus pandemic will bring new challenges. We must ensure that the rights-based approach stays on the agenda. We need to reinforce the message that our lives and experiences have equal value to those of other citizens; this is one of the constant challenges we face. Another challenge facing people is the prospect of being stuck in day-care centres, and there may be a reluctance on the part of staff to change this culture, as they run the risk of unemployment.

In addition we need to broaden our focus and become involved in other human rights movements so that disabled people are adequately represented within these spaces. People must feel safe to share their opinions, and we need to come to a shared realisation that we are not working against each other. We need to embrace the psychosocial model and move away from the stigmatising label of "mental health". We have the same rights as other citizens but we may need support to access them, whether those supports are personal assistance, technological or others.

Selina Bonnie

I fell into the world of activism. I didn't identify as a disabled person until my late teens or early twenties, even though I have been a wheelchair user since I was ten. I didn't want to be seen as a disabled person. I didn't even want to be seen with other disabled people. Like many disabled people, my childhood was peppered with experiences of being manhandled by professionals and physios. My mother was a fantastic woman who always wanted what was best for me but believed that the only way to be independent was me having the ability to do things for myself, including having the ability to walk.

I worked in the music industry and then I worked on a Community Employment scheme for an arts and disability organisation from 1993 to 1996. In January 2002 I assumed the role of access officer for South Dublin County Council, a role I hold to this day. I had colleagues who identified as being part of the

LGBT community, and also colleagues who had dys-
lexia. Although they were in an arts organisation, they
were starting to put disability and sexuality together.
I also became involved with John Gormley, who was
the Mayor of Dublin at the time, and the Green movement. My interactions with such a diverse range of
people inspired me to run Ireland's first disability and
sexuality conference in the Mansion House, which was
entitled All Different, All Sexual in 1995. Although it
was a huge success, there was still a little bit of pushback
against it. However, this was something I wanted to be
a part of and add my voice to. I wasn't overly surprised
to learn that people with disabilities are often infantil-
ised when it comes to sexuality – sometimes disabled
people are seen as being incapable and vulnerable. A
key moment was when I read a book called *The Sexual
Politics of Disability*. It occurred to me that if people
needed assistance with personal care, then they would
also need assistance in exploring their sexuality.

Like many disabled people, my own perception of
disability stemmed from a childhood characterised by
the intervention of medical professionals. However, in
1995 I met a man who would change my mind for-
ever. Fianna Fáil were launching their manifesto in the

Davenport Hotel. Out of nowhere this man in a hat I'd never met before flew into the room in his power-chair. There was this sense that the king had arrived. Even the highest-ranking politician seemed to respect him. I remember thinking, *Who is that?* It was Martin Naughton. Never before had I seen somebody in a wheelchair command so much power. I learned from Martin that having control over your life was more important than having the physical ability to do things. Martin Naughton and Joe T. Mooney then took me under their wing.

Fast forward to a year later, and I was working for Martin in public affairs in an office in Parnell Square. That was before we moved to the iconic gate lodge at Carmichael House, North Brunswick Street. I often sat on the floor at midnight to make placards to be used at Martin's many "actions" (we were not allowed to call them protests) and made many flasks of tea for people who were protesting outside the Dáil. I had the opportunity to work with people I considered to be some of the great influencers of the time, including Christian O'Reilly, Dermot Walsh, Joe T. Mooney and John Doyle. John was a wordsmith, the master of the slo-gan, such was his command of words. He could also turn politicians' slogans back on them. I remember in particular the protests he held outside Heuston Station, trying to make transport companies such as Irish Rail, Bus Éireann and Dublin Bus make their services more accessible. These people taught me that having a personal assistant was about being in control of my own life. I loved the camaraderie and having the craic.

Through the Centre for Independent Living, I became a trainer in equality through NUI Maynooth. I did my final assignment on disability and sexuality. I also studied sexual equality in Leeds University, where Professor Colin Barnes supervised my dissertation entitled "Facilitating Sexual Expression Within the Independent Living Movement in Ireland". After this I lectured on sexuality at the summer school in Santander, Spain. Subsequently I was invited to write a chapter on disability and sexuality for a book on those topics in Ireland, published by University College Cork. It took many months to complete but it was a great achievement.

In terms of having a family, I've always thought of myself as a sexual, maternal being. Sadly I would describe myself as a survivor of the reproductive health system. My journey into motherhood was not an easy one. Adoption was a brick wall, so we decided to go down the IVF route, which was gruelling. My daughter was born after fifteen years; she was my fourth pregnancy. One of the top doctors presented us with a load of questions that he wanted answers to, and he wanted a cast-iron guarantee that my child would not be born with an impairment. There was also the usual assumption that because I couldn't "run after" my child I would somehow be less of a parent. Although I proved them wrong, I was surprised at how my own perceptions could be challenged. In 2012 the BBC filmed a documentary called *We Won't Drop the Baby*, which follows the birth of comedian Laurence Clark and his wife Adele's second son, Jamie. Both Laurence and Adele have cerebral palsy. When Laurence picked up his son by grabbing his babygrow, it made me consider how creative disabled parents can be in navigating parenting roles.

I am a regional ambassador with the Re(al) Productive Justice project, which is an initiative of the Centre of Disability Law and Policy in NUI Galway. Although it's not as unusual for disabled people to become parents today, many improvements are needed to make life easier for disabled parents. Maternity units are still inaccessible in many ways. I've heard so many negative stories, including of children being removed from parents because of a lack of adequate supports. For example, it's only recently that deaf parents have access to a sign language interpreter at the birth of their child. Some things have improved, but we still have some way to go, which is why the project is so important. For example, baby-changing areas in public spaces are often not accessible to me and other wheelchair-using parents. This remains the case across the country, but I'm proud to say that through my work, changing areas are becoming more accessible to all parents in south Dublin.

Although some aspects of my parenting and activism journey have been difficult, being disabled is a central part of my identity. It has made me more solution-focused and has encouraged me to become more inclusive, not only in relation to things like facilitating physical access through ramps, but also in areas like Braille signage and loop systems in public spaces. I'm also proud of how my daughter has embraced my intersectionality and how this has made her more open-minded.

However, there is still work to do in terms of rights. Personal belief, lobbying and activism are key, but at some stage you need to become the changemaker yourself. This change can often be brought about through collaboration with local authorities and by using structures that are already in place, such as the Public Sector Duty, which could be used to advance the rights of disabled people. I love my job because I feel that I can make real change. When I joined South Dublin County Council in 2001, we established the social inclusion unit, which I managed for four years. From there I moved into the area of access, taking on the disability access brief at a time when the government was allocating money to improve accessibility. I've taken on the role of access officer, which gives me the opportunity to work with every sector of the council. I'm also part of various national networks. Some people are set in their ways, while others are open to change. If you can speak to architects and planners in their own language, real progress can be made. They like to look good, which is a trick that I've learned.

Overall I think people just want more control over their lives. I also feel we need to be more solution-focused. Being a wheelchair user has opened my mind and strengthened my lateral thinking skills. I am proud of the diversity and intersectionality within our family, and of how my daughter doesn't see difference – she just sees people.

We also need to be mindful that too many people are stealing human rights language but not living the meaning of it. Social media can be a powerful tool in projecting the message of equality and rights.

I feel quietly optimistic about the future. I believe that the Covid-19 pandemic could act as a catalyst in bringing about positive change for disabled people. At a time when the emphasis is on social distancing, pavements will need to be widened and public spaces made accessible. It has made employers more open to people working from home, which I hope will present more opportunities for disabled people to access employment. Ultimately real change can only happen when those with lived experiences work in collaboration with policy makers to advance the rights of disabled people.

Jacqui Browne

I was born and reared in Co. Kerry. I identify as a thalidomide survivor as opposed to a "thalidomide victim". My early childhood involved a lot of hospitalisations and surgeries, and I was a source of wonder to the medical establishment. I also experienced long periods of time away from my family, in hospital or residential settings. Back in the sixties, it took nearly seven hours to get from Kerry to Dublin by car or on a train, which meant that if you were in hospital for long periods, you had no visitors. I was on my own, on the flat of my back, being turned every four hours. The psychological impact of that was never understood. However, these experiences shaped me in many ways into the person I am and made me very independent.

I feel that a lot of my experience comes from a "deficit model" approach. Assessments centred around what I could not do; there were never any assessments focusing on what I could do or what I could do with support or a piece of equipment. A lot of childhood assessments were deficit orientated. From occupational therapists, physiotherapists, the nursing profession and the medical profession, everything was "the poor cratur" model as I call it. I still get the patronising "aren't you great" spiel sometimes. I grew up with that model of being "great", "an inspiration" and "wonderful".

My experience of education until I was eighteen years of age was haphazard. I now understand that the education system failed me as opposed to me failing within that system. We had no internet, technology or any of the access facilities that we have nowadays. I attended boarding school for a short time, which I enjoyed immensely, but because of a lack of accessibility, I had to leave. I officially failed my Leaving Certificate as I did not pass Irish, which at that time was a requirement. Following my very poor Leaving Certificate exam results, a vocational officer at the National Rehabilitation Board (NRB), recommended that I do a secretarial course, which again seemed to draw on the deficit model; the misperception was that I'd make a "good little secretary". I rebelled against it, and this lit a fire inside me to stand up for my rights.

Following a short stint on the secretarial course, I successfully applied for a position in banking, where I spent ten years of my first career. I enjoyed it and it was a great time for me in many ways. I gained my independence and started driving. After a while I got a transfer from Limerick to Dublin, where I undertook a bachelor of arts degree (five evenings a week after work) at University College Dublin. During that time in Dublin, I became more aware of who I was and where I stood in society. I always had a problem with rattling the charity boxes on the streets. In those days it was very much "help the handicapped" and I was uncomfortable with that. I started searching for a different model and I came across a name: Donal Toolan. I made it my business to meet up with Donal, as well as Maureen McGovern, Michael Fox, Steve Daunt and Dermot Hayes, at various junctures during the early nineties. We became a powerhouse.

I then got involved in the Forum of People with Disabilities. There were huge discussions as well as healthy arguments. These were important because as a collective we were teasing out our understanding of the various models of disability. We hadn't really yet got the language but we were clear about our rights. Donal was streets ahead of all of us. He was challenging at times, which I thought was great. In the early days of the Forum, we kept it simple. Our first campaign was the right to vote for disabled people.

In the early days of the Centre for Independent Living, Martin Naughton and an American lady called Jana Overbo started a campaign called Operation Get Out. We were challenging people, particularly at government level, to get people out of institutions. We took over hotel foyers, the Mansion House, Government Buildings, and protested outside the Dáil. It was incredible and a testament to those original leaders of the movement.

The response to the voting campaign was positive. I think we made some government officials uncomfortable and they didn't know how to deal with us. The Department of the Environment was responsible for enabling people to exercise their right to vote. The postal vote was seen as the panacea, a way of appeasing us and keeping us in our little boxes. Frustratingly we felt that people did not understand what we were asking for.

Maintaining connections with other activists had its challenges. It was the early nineties: the internet was in its infancy, and there was no such thing as graphics or sharing articles. Nonetheless the Forum was good at connecting people. The membership was small, which helped, but it was a grassroots membership, which I think is critical. The Forum was focused, and we set out an objective to secure the establishment of a Commission on the Status of People with Disabilities in Ireland, which we secured in 1993. The Commission was established by Mervyn Taylor TD, the Minister for Equality and Law Reform, and its report, *A Strategy for Equality*, was published in 1996. This report was significant. Before its publication, there had been few inquiries or conversations about the rights of people with disabilities, and the establishment of the Commission marked an important milestone in rectifying this. Although we didn't finish the report within the originally allocated two-year time frame, it was the first step towards discussing disability in a rights-based context. The report sets out 402 recommendations in total. While some of these recommendations are obsolete now, others may be worth exploring in the context of the UNCPRD in the future.

In terms of keeping the movement going, I think we need to identify champions, not only within our movement but outside of ourselves as well. If we get caught up exclusively in a "nothing about us without us" approach, we will lose out as a movement. We need allies. President Mary Robinson was a wonderful champion for disabled people and their rights. Mervyn Taylor also did tremendous work with the Forum, and it was through him that the Forum secured the establishment of the Commission on the Rights of People with Disabilities. A couple of years after the publication of *A Strategy for Equality*, the Forum decided to close down. We had achieved our mission.

I think the momentum of activism can be hugely sustained within the wider NGO sector. We have made huge progress and I believe this can be sustained with allies from other human rights organisations and other like-minded groups working on various issues. On paper we may have made progress officially, but practical progress is slow. But I do think the sector is more able to cope with what I would call "tactile" changes like building regulations. For example, take Part M and the principles of universal design – people can get stuck into those and send engineers out to upgrade our building regulations. We can bring about physical changes, but getting the more hidden but really important social issues addressed can be much harder, and while we certainly have made progress, I think we have quite a bit to go still.

In the 1990s the government decided to foist upon us a national organisation of disabled people, as opposed to facilitating the development of a grassroots organisation. We were presented with the National Council for People with Disabilities, and in my view, the model was wrong from the start. It was a top-down approach, and we were given an official who was an employee in the Department of Justice to act as a CEO. It never really took off. Later on, the model of People with Disabilities in Ireland (PWDI) constituted an effort to develop a grassroots-type organisation. However, it was still controlled by a government department. I don't think there was enough groundwork done to allow that model to flourish.

One of the reasons this model failed was that there wasn't enough clarity among ourselves as disabled people. People were coming together who'd never met in their lives, who had never considered their own grassroots. This model was being imposed on people who were then expected to work together. Just look at women's groups, Travellers' groups – those groups grew from the bottom up. We did not do this.

We need to create opportunities for DPOs to come together for pieces of work that are common to all of us. I think DPOs need to stay focused on the task when they come together. If we genuinely care about the rights of disabled people, we need to ensure that no one is left behind. if we stay focused on that, people will recognise that this is not only about ourselves but also about future generations.

I think a grassroots organisation is the ideal, and I know that some DPOs already have a good grassroots or active membership. However, I think we have neither the capacity nor the funding for any one group or organisation to address all the issues facing disabled people. At least thirteen and a half per cent of the population have a disability and it's a lie to pretend that any one group of us can produce a single, genuine grassroots organisation. The way this country operates, we're probably better off looking to any number of genuine DPOs to make their best effort at developing a grassroots organisation around the issues that concern disabled people. And then maybe the best way to go forward is to look at how these organisations can work together on issues of common concern, for example the UNCRPD. For me a DPO is guided, led and directed by disabled people. All actions, strategies and opinions are guided by the vast majority of people within that organisation. That is not to say that people won't need support from others outside the organisation, people who might not have a disability. But the situation at the moment is that we have a lot of disability organisations, especially disability service providers, that claim to represent us but are not run or directed by us.

In a true DPO we are not clients.

We are the organisation.

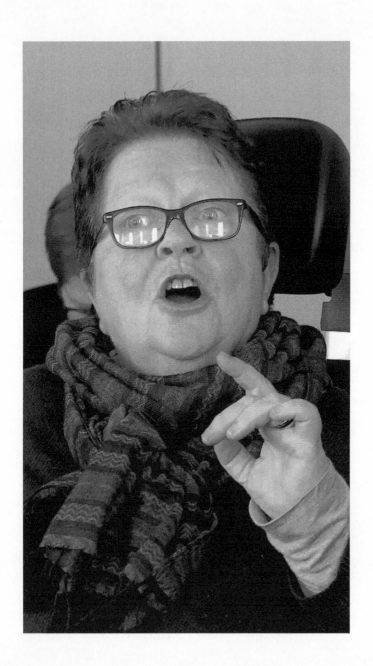

Maureen McGovern

I was born in 1957 and contracted polio in 1958. I got the "itis" part, which left me disabled. As a result I spent fourteen years in the orthopaedic clinic in Clontarf, and then I moved to the Central Remedial Clinic, where I was put into second class at the age of fourteen. I come from a background of poverty, where there were problems including violence and alcoholism. The social worker's solution was to move me into an institution. The experience of living in hospitals was institutionalising, and I am still quite institutionalised in many ways. Nonetheless it was a relief not to be at home. My mother was one of my role models. She was a fighter. She separated from my father, which wasn't done at the time, and fought to get each member of my family into safe spaces.

I was allowed home twice a year – a week during the summer and a week at Christmas – but I always dreaded it. I considered the disabled people in the home to be my family. When I was eighteen, I started attending Ballymun Comprehensive. All my classmates were eleven or twelve. I left after a year because the whole experience was just horrendous.

After Ballymun I did a secretarial course with Rehab in Sligo, after which I got my own flat in Dublin at the age of nineteen. Having spent so much of my time in institutional settings, it came as a shock to learn how inaccessible the real world was, and to face the negative attitudes and discrimination that I had been somewhat protected from. Although I loved my independence, I began to miss being around other disabled people, especially women and the sense of sisterhood they provided.

I worked as a telephonist and from there I became involved in the Disabled Persons Action Group, which was set up by Tommy Gallagher in Ballymun. As a group we focused on three things: the Cheshire Home, securing the postal vote and sheltered workshops. We started visiting the Cheshire Home in the Phoenix Park and we met a guy there called Richard Mooney, a really strong advocate. From talking to him, we discovered that the residents of the home were going to bed at eight o'clock at night and getting up whenever they were told to. There was no mobility allowance at the time, so they couldn't even go for a night out. A relationship developed between Richard and another woman, which wasn't allowed. We fought for Richard to represent residents on the board. We fought for the mobility allowance (which was later scrapped) for these residents so that they could go out at least once a month. Wheelchair users would also get stuck in the cattle grids, so we got them removed.

At that time Nora Draper had taken a case against the constitution about not being able to vote at home. She won her case. A special voters' list allowed disabled people to vote at home, but there had to be a presiding officer and a garda in your home while you were voting if you couldn't access the polling station. We fought to have these requirements abolished, and now disabled people can avail of a postal vote. Combat Poverty gave us their offices to work from and also some money under the table.

The Disabled Persons in Action Group spoke to people working in sheltered workshops. At the time many disabled people were coming from special education backgrounds and there wasn't a lot of work available to disabled people. The idea behind the sheltered workshops was that disabled people would work on consumer goods – lamps, in-flight

meals for Aer Lingus – things that the economy would benefit from. The disabled person didn't benefit from this, of
course. Most of them were working five days a week, to
a standard in line with their ability. Whatever they earned
would then be handed back to the institution, and the disabled person received a weekly allowance of between £1
and £5. They had no protection, no union rights.

We started looking across the water to Mike Barrett
from the National League of the Blind and Disabled
in England. Martin Hogan, the chairperson of the
Waterford Action Group, and I were invited over, and
we visited seven times to look at their unions and the
set-up of their workshops. Then we decided to hold a
conference and invite disabled people who were working in the workshops. We discussed how to go about
unionising the workshops over here. We invited a member of the National Rehabilitation Board (NRB) who
was a trade unionist, as well as other guest speakers,
such as a person from the workshops and people from
prisoners' action groups. We even went on an afternoon
show on television. The representative from the NRB
was brought into the office the day before the conference was due to take place and was told that if she spoke
at the conference, she would be fired. Tom O'Connor

told us what had happened and he gave her speech that day. Disabled people were also told that if they went to the conference, they too would be fired. Martin and I wrote a book on that experience.

Looking back, one mistake we made was that we didn't share our information with others, or bring people along with us. I joined other groups, like H Block and prisoners' rights groups, to see how they ran their campaigns. I heard about a meeting in Trinity College, where Donal Toolan was starting something. Disabled people were going to start campaigning for change. I became involved in the Forum of People with Disabilities and loved it. I really liked that there were different intellects coming into that. Jacqui Browne and others were good at the policy side of things. Everybody had a part to play in the whole disability movement, no matter what their interests were. It also brought disabled people together.

Because of my experiences around violence and rape, I wanted to work in the disability sector, particularly from a human rights perspective. I worked for People with Disabilities Ireland (PWDI) as a network worker, working from Kerry to Dublin. I met many disabled women in this role, some of whom were experiencing horrendously violent circumstances in their homes. They didn't know where to turn, who to talk to. Disabled women were not being believed. Some were being oppressed by non-disabled men. I had a conversation with a friend of mine from Women's Aid about finding support for disabled women. Where could they ring if they wanted to get out or wanted to be supported in a refuge? We were told, "We don't get many disabled people ringing up." In response we set up a Disabled Women's Working Group and worked together to see what we could do to create a space to support disabled women. We worked with them for two years, during which time they moved to an accessible building. We held educational workshops for disabled women, exploring the meaning of violence and what could be done.

In addition, a research piece was commissioned to see how many disabled women in Ireland were victims of violence. The researchers were only interested if we included information about violence against men. I was more interested in exploring violence against disabled women, as this seemed to happen more frequently than against men. Women's Aid and the National Disability Authority held a seminar together. I would really like to work with Women's Aid again as I think violence against disabled women is an important issue.

After my work with Women's Aid, I fancied another change. I began to consider whether, after working all my life, I could afford to live exclusively on Disability Allowance, and I could – if I gave up smoking, drinking and my car. I wanted to do something locally in Ballyfermot. I was invited by Catherine Lane to attend an access group meeting. We also set up a drama group called Smashing Barriers. It gave disabled people interested in producing, acting or writing a chance to come together. We took a cross-impairment approach; there was no discrimination. We came to our own conclusions about what disability was. We wrote a play addressing the issue of disabled people being inappropriately placed in nursing homes. It was a political piece looking at how the government was beginning to institutionalise disabled people. In Portland, Oregon, in the US, everything you needed to participate in society – access, sign language – was in place. We wrote the play as a collective, and it was well received within the Ballyfermot area. We were asked to perform the play in Tallaght and Ballymun. The entire group – bar one person – was made up of disabled people. Everything was based on the social model of disability but we were really aware of the medical model as well. Now we are working on another play about Covid-19, and we also brought Peter Kearns in to do a bit of work on a piece called "Unfair City". Peter did a fantastic job in highlighting how unfair things are for disabled people in Dublin.

We needed Smashing Barriers to hang out as a group, so we got rid of the access group tag and in its place used "disability action collective". Doing this allowed us to explore disability through other mediums such as debate and creative writing. We are also discussing the possibility of setting up a choir. Others want to explore disability from an academic point of view. We want to become stronger as leaders in our community, and we are mentoring each other and sharing skills to ensure we pass on critical information.

I live in accordance with the social model of disability. I believe that there are barriers getting in the way of what I want to do and that these barriers need to be broken down. We need to demand that these barriers are removed for all disabled people. I have a right to be here; I have respect for myself. It took a while to get here; I hated myself for years and didn't think I deserved to be here, but that was due to all the negative attitudes coming at me that told me I was worthless when I am not. I have a lot to give and this is why I am drawn to the community development principles

– working as a collective and sharing information. Once people build themselves up, nothing can bring them down.

Moving forward, we need to work with disabled people on the ground and reach out in every way possible. We need to find where disabled people are and provide peer support first, and then pick the road we want to travel on as a collective. Disabled people must build capacity with each other and must be employed at disabled people's organisations. If we are not confident enough to keep fighting, we will never have legislation in place to protect our rights.

Peter Kearns

I always joke that although I have gone to Lourdes, taken medication and have been to many doctors, I cannot be cured – nothing can be done about my Dublin accent.

I grew up in East Wall and then Coolock, on a working-class estate, in a house provided by Dublin Corporation. My parents had the confidence to challenge the medical community at a time when many disabled children were kept behind closed doors "for their own protection". In the nineties, disabled people started going to mainstream school, but I think one disadvantage of mainstreaming is that we missed the opportunity to create a strong disability movement.

I availed of the special school system during the sixties and seventies. Every day I was collected by bus and brought to a special school in Sandymount, until I was twelve. At the age of nine I remember watching a programme on BBC called *Joey*, which was about a young boy with cerebral palsy whose happy ending was gaining a place in a local special school. After watching it, my dad turned to me and said, "You're going to have to change this narrative." At the time I didn't have many disabled mentors to look up to.

Before I left Sandymount, I remember the journeys to school on the bus and in particular going past Trinity College. This was around the time that the Church lifted the ban on Catholics attending Trinity, in the early seventies. I remember looking at the building, admiring its magnificence, and thinking, *One day I will go there.* I said this to my friend Paul, who went on to manage the paralympic football team. Someone from the back of the bus advised me to keep my aspirations to myself if I didn't want to be examined by the psychiatrist in Sandymount. This was the same psychiatrist who told me that I couldn't be taught to read and write. As far as they were concerned, my future involved workshops and day-care centres.

I attended Sandymount until the age of twelve when I escaped to Ballymun Comprehensive. This was the first school in the country that was made accessible to disabled students. I remember it was much bigger than what I was accustomed to – there were 300 boys in first year. One of my friends who had epilepsy also went to Ballymun but ended up back in Sandymount because he found it too tough. That scared the shite out of me – I didn't know you could be sent back! However, there were some great teachers in the school at the time. After the Inter Cert I dropped art and focused on English. The threat of being sent back to Sandymount was ever-present in the background, even at that stage.

I studied computer applications for two years at DCU, from 1983. I was the first disabled student in the college. I was led to believe by the career guidance teacher in Sandymount that it would lead to great job prospects. I dropped out and I got my opportunity to go to Trinity in 1986 to study English. My parents thought that they couldn't just walk into Trinity, given our working-class background, so I always appreciated the opportunity to study there. It was a brilliant experience. I used it as an opportunity to improve my writing and I got the chance to read all the classics. I only realise now how profound an experience it was. It was on the back of my degree that I got an opportunity to work in the Abbey Theatre for three years. It wasn't my cup of tea, though, and instead I chose to focus on forum theatre, working with working-class and community groups. It occurred to me that I could wed two different interests – my love of drama and the social model – into a vehicle that would promote change and awareness. I could use a cultural, creative approach to changing the disability narrative.

It was during this time – the 1980s – that I began to consider disability from a political perspective. I met many people at this time who became mentors. I was influenced by Marxism to start looking at disability as a social and political issue. During the late eighties I started learning about the social model of disability, which for me opened the gates to an understanding of disability beyond human charity. Suddenly the focus was not on impairment but sign language, Braille and physical access. Our obsession with labels fascinates me, because there was a time when impairment was merely a part of the human condition. For example, prior to Dr Little's "discovery" of cerebral palsy in 1853 it had no label, and in the early days following its discovery, it was just known as Little's disease. I met Christy Brown, and although I respected him there was always a sense of pity and charity about him. I was looking for something different. I was looking for social change.

In 1990 I finished my English degree and was embarking on a HDip in education, when I was approached by Donal Toolan to contribute to the Forum of People with Disabilities. At the time I was chairing an access group at Trinity College, which was going strong. This felt like a good opportunity to promote the social model. However, I felt that the forum was not tied enough to the political system at the time. The 1996 report published by the Commission on the Status of People with Disabilities, is still so relevant today. The fact that it referred to "people with disabilities" as opposed to "disabled people" led me to question whether the forum had fully understood the social model.

The forum understood the value of a creative approach. In 1996 myself, Donal and others created a drama course for people who had Asperger's and ADHD, in Peamount Hospital.

The forum also did a lot of work around intellectual disability as well as physical and sensory disability, which empowered people to ask about their rights, such as their right to Disability Allowance and the right to choose their own clothes. Paul Alford is a great example of someone with an intellectual disability who wrote his autobiography and now lives independently. During the Celtic Tiger years, we started to explore how we value disabled people. We set up a cabaret starring disabled people and explored the affirmation model through these performances.

Around this time I began to consider what brought disabled people together. What did we have in common? I think that once we recognise that it's barriers that disable us, then we share common ground. For me an impairment is an individual experience, whereas embracing the social model allows us to build a collective. I also felt that, in order to be effective, there needed to be an academic element to the disability movement, which led me to become a lecturer in disability studies in Sligo. Part of my role was establishing the Irish Disability Studies Association. I felt the need for a social model academic structure, so that disabled people could enter that space, share their personal experiences, and then use the space to build a movement. The social model is also the start of us being recognised as having rights under the UNCRPD.

In 2019 three major plays exploring disability were staged, but not one of these featured a disabled actor. Disability is still portrayed through the lens of individual tragedy, as well as impairment. Impairment overshadows everything – disabled characters are rarely explored in an intersectional way. Would it be acceptable for someone to "black up" to play Othello? Then why is it okay to use non-disabled actors to play disabled characters? Having authentic disabled actors changes the whole production.

To promote the social model, we need to first acknowledge the medical/charity model and explore why it is so strong. "People with disabilities" is a medical term but the social model says that we are "disabled people". The fact is that disability is an industry and we are cash cows. The disability sector is a business. We have to cost impairment, but ultimately someone else owns the value of disability. That's why we are obsessed with labels in the disability sector – because they bring in money – to the tune of €2 billion a year. My cerebral palsy has a fiscal value, and that's why we need to deconstruct the medical model. Impairment labels aren't all bad, though; sometimes they can be used to one's advantage. It was having a label of cerebral palsy that enabled me to access the supports I needed to achieve my educational qualifications and to "escape" when my friends could not. As far as I know, Scotland is the only country that has the social model of disability written into its constitution.

There have been several attempts to establish a disabled people's organisation (DPO) since the Forum of People with Disabilities disbanded in 2007. In my view a true DPO promotes intersectionality. The Independent Living Movement Ireland (ILMI) is the only organisation I know of that is trying to build a movement and a collective that is cross-impairment, that focuses on capacity-building and bringing people together across class and gender as well. I think we need platforms such as the one being provided by ILMI to discuss our issues, as these can bring about real change. Admittedly this isn't as "sexy" as marching, though. I remember going to lots of marches and protests during the eighties, but nothing was ever really achieved. For me the key is having a strong organisation behind us. I am impressed with how ILMI is using virtual platforms at a time of crisis to keep members connected as a collective.

I have always been wary of tokenism. In my view tokenism is a way of stopping radical disabled activists getting into power. Even insisting that disabled people must have places on the board of any organisation is tokenism in my view. I also don't agree with labels, and for me a movement cannot be based on impairment. It must be embedded in the principles of the social model.

Ann Marie Flanagan

I was born in October 1972, the third of four children. My older sister Fidelma died when she was six months old – three months before I was born. I grew up between two boys. My birth wasn't viewed as a tragedy; given my parents' devastating loss, they were glad that I was going to live and be okay. As a young child I spent extended periods in the Croom Hospital in County Limerick. Being away from my parents and brothers was a regular occurrence, which as a young child, was very upsetting. My parents could only visit for two hours on a Sunday.

I grew up on a council housing estate in the rural Clare area of Corofin village. We lived across from the local primary school. My older brother and a neighbouring older child carried me to school every day before I got a pushchair. One of my first non-family role models was the principal of the national school, Declan Kelleher. I experienced in primary school what we understand today as the social model. He was determined to meet the needs of all of his students. For example, he organised a fundraiser so that an access ramp could be built at the entrance. I remember telling him how excited I was that the ramp was for me. And his response was, the ramp was for everyone – ensuring that I wasn't seeing myself as 'special' or in any way less than the others. I was facilitated in sport, singing, acting and other activities, on an equal basis to other children, which gave me confidence and self-belief.

At the age of seven I wanted to join a step-dancing class in Corofin. I asked my mother for the fifty pence fee, which she gave me, not asking how I thought I was going to participate, which I did – every week for five years. I was never held back by my family. I went to the classes and the dance teacher, Lily Slevin, would get two other children to hold my hands so I could take part. A year later there was an opportunity to compete in a Feis. The teacher was taken aback when I asked to be registered. To distract me, the following week she presented me with a medal, thinking that I would be placated and not want to compete. She was wrong: I competed. When I wasn't announced as taking third or second place, I felt so sure I was going to win. I did! I was joint first, and I remember the place erupted in applause when I went on stage. I asked my mam, 'Was I that good? No one else had that reaction'.

For the first twelve years of my life, I felt equal to the other children. I was about ten when I met a disabled woman who was my occupational therapist. I wanted to be like her – she was married and had kids. Around the same time, I got my first mobility aid that I could move independently in – a hand trike. It gave me so much independence.

The year I turned thirteen was quite a traumatic one in my life. My uncle Pat died young, which was devastating for my mother, grandparents and for all of us. My family moved from the village into the country, and I started secondary school. Starting secondary school was a dehumanising experience, and it was assumed that I was somehow intellectually inferior. Initially, some family members found it difficult to accept that I'd started using a wheelchair, convinced by medical professionals that I would lose my existing mobility if I used it, and become less 'able'. This soon changed when we all enjoyed the liberation that having a wheelchair afforded me. As I grew, I also disliked constantly having to ask Mam for help with personal support, always feeling I was putting her out. They were great parents; puberty and being a teenager made me more aware and self-conscious and I felt that they had other things to do. I naturally wanted to be more independent, just like my peers.

In recalling the shoots of my budding activism, on a summer camp for young disabled people, come half past eight, the volunteers would attempt to put us to bed. I was a sixteen-year-old who was into typical teenage things. I spoke up and challenged the volunteers about people with higher support needs being put to bed so early. I reminded them that this was our holiday. We had a ball after that and felt triumph in our advocacy. Some of the adults were not happy as this interrupted a good night's partying.

I became involved in a national disability organisation. Although it was based on the charity model, at branch level it was great craic. The two women who organised the branch retired, and after that the branch was then run almost entirely by disabled people. I took over as secretary and other members assumed the roles of chairperson and treasurer. We invited our non-disabled friends and siblings to become volunteer drivers and helpers (as they were called then), for example. This way of working introduced me to the "nothing about us without us" mantra.

In 1991 the Association for Higher Education Access and Disability (AHEAD) was established. I was the rep for Tralee Regional Technical College, where I studied Computer Programming. It opened my eyes to rights-based activism. College was liberating. I made the most of my freedom, with "extracurricular activities" taking up a great deal of my time. My interest in computer science was low and it was not to be my career.

When I first went to college, I had no personal assistance and only a manual wheelchair. I had become used to non-family assisting me. My mother helped me onto the bus and my landlady helped me off the bus. On the first day, I asked someone to push me to and from college. Three days later the lovely landlady asked me if this was my plan for the rest of college. She suggested a motorised chair. The medical model was so ingrained in me that I believed that using an motorised chair would be a backwards step. At the time there was a benevolent fund for students who couldn't pay rent. So not to have me at the centre of a charity event, the plan was to raise money for the motorised chair and top up the fund. The Students' Union got involved, and I became a "celebrity" for a year. One day I went to the canteen to find about 2,000 students there along with a band. I was the guest of honour and they presented me with the chair. It changed my life! I remember the feelings of equality and autonomy with someone walking beside me for the first time – it was surreal.

Around this time, Dermot Hayes reached out to me wanting to address the lack of rights of disabled people. Dermot was involved in the Clare Community Co-op on the outskirts of Corofin. When I got involved this collective approach gave me the analysis and language I needed to understand and articulate the many political, social and economic barriers experienced by so many in society including disabled people, which translates to the social model of disability. Dermot, Donnacha Rynne, Thomas Connole, Declan Considine and myself, the only woman, co-founded the Disabled People of Clare (DPOC). We also formed part of the Clare Network for Disadvantaged Communities, working with other groups who experience inequality. A key mentor in my early activism was Michael Neylon, sociologist and co-founder of the Co-op.

Other groups we networked with were people parenting alone, members of the Traveller Community, and

women who had reared their families and weren't entitled
to a contributory pension. As a collective of issue-based
communities we applied for EU structural funding,
where the criteria was responding to area-based disadvantage. This exercise enabled us to change State policy,
recognising the deprivation people experienced based on
our identity. It was important to address those common
issues which reduced the siloed approached to disabled
people and other groups, e.g. the Traveller community.

At that time, in the early 1990s, there was collective
action in the movement sprouting up in other parts of
the country. The Forum of People with Disabilities and
the Centre for Independent Living (CIL) were also in
their infancy. In Clare, we were hungry to be part of
the wider movement. The DPOC drew on the constitution of the Forum of People with Disabilities. Donal
Toolin (RIP) became one of my close friends and life
teachers. We met Martin Naughton (RIP) for the first
time and we invited him to Clare. The irony of it, as it
was a fundraiser. Martin quickly offered us an opportunity to consider what "Rights not Charity" fully meant!
Learning about the Independent Living Movement
(ILM) allowed us to be politically active. Our first campaign was to call on the National Rehabilitation Board

(NRB) to make their premises accessible as it had steps into the office. Consequently, the regional manager became an ally and granted us seed funding.

When we were establishing the Personal Assistance Service (PAS) in Clare, it struck me how afraid people were of stepping away from dependency on family, and so too were those families. The notion of a stranger coming into people's homes and providing intimate support was very confronting. With Martin Naughton's support and our persuasiveness we secured a FÁS Community Employment scheme. Dermot was the appointed as supervisor and I took on role of administrator, blending the two wages and sharing the responsibilities. We knocked on people's doors, explained the role of a Personal Assistance Service, asking if they would like to try it. A lot of the original Leaders were married women with children. Three Leaders had acquired disabilities and were experiencing domestic abuse. Having a Personal Assistant changed their lives, changed all our lives. The co-operative approach was aligned to the DPOC values and philosophy. We were about sharing resources such as transport and skills. With the expansion of the DPOC in terms of new members, demands from funders and pressure to be centrally located, we moved to Ennis.

Dermot and I found moving from Roxton into Ennis difficult as we knew we were losing a core part of our support network. When we opened DPOC up to all disabled people, it was quickly evident that many disabled people in society were still entrenched in the charity model. The founders were losing our grip on the rights-based model.

In 1996 I moved to Dublin first as a Programme Manager with CIL and then to Co-ordinator of Interact, Specialist Support Agency within the Community Development Programme for three and a half years. During this time, I met Nick Danagher (RIP) from Surrey, UK, at an international conference we organised here in Ireland on PAS. This afforded me the opportunity to move to the UK as a Direct Payments Advisor. I also received a direct payment myself, which was a life changing and wonderful experience. The entire process was led by disabled people. The organisation, which was a DPO, was contracted by the Local Authority's Social Services to provide support and direct payments advice.

I returned to Ireland in 2001 to follow my heart with Derek. I felt there was so much to be done at home. The UK had a strong legislative framework that we didn't have here. I wanted to bring my knowledge home, reconnect with the movement and support the DPOC. An action of the DPOC was to peer support people to write to the housing section to secure local authority housing, and to the HSE for PAS. At an organisational level we campaigned for all housing developments to include accessible housing. This was hugely successful. In Corofin, back to my roots, I secured a house where I lived for twelve years (and my son, Robert, was born into that home). Independent Living Community Services was looking for a National Development Officer. Joe T. Mooney (RIP), the manager at the time, interviewed and offered me the position. I supported the work of CILs throughout the country and coordinated the NUI Maynooth Disability Studies programme.

After this, West Limerick CIL and the Cheshire Home contracted me to develop a Disability Equality training programme and deliver it. From here I applied for a job with Shine, supporting recovery of people with mental-health challenges and family members, and I have been working there for eighteen years.

I've also been involved in politics over the years. I joined a political party and ran for local election twice, was vice-chair to their national executive, involved in policy development, and part of an election task-force.

I first contested in 2004 and it was an opportunity to influence the minds of people who saw disabled people as a single-issue candidate. Climate change, social justice, inclusion, participatory democracy were and are core to my politics. In the 2009 local elections the number of seats in the constituency reduced from six to five and, alas, I just lost out.

In 2011 my son was born – a moment I'd waited for my whole life. I had an income, a partner and a Personal Assistant Service. However, my bubble burst on returning home on 24 July, when I received a letter from the HSE stating that they were cutting thirty of my PA hours. I had written to the HSE and PA service provider before my child's birth telling them I was to become a mother. Each agency put the decision to cut my hours on each other. During this time I felt quite alone. I learned, however, that many other disabled people were having the same experience. Those people had no one to speak up for them, and so I organised meetings. I and a few others managed to protect our PA hours. Campaigning while on maternity leave was distressing and demeaned my dignity. I needed to support myself and others. I had stepped back from DPOC. It disbanded soon after owing to funding changes and cuts. While it felt shocking at the time, it was the best decision. It was no longer about rights and independent living.

In August 2012 there was an announcement that the Personal Assistant budget would be slashed by €10 million. Fellow activists slept outside the Dáil in protest. I was in campaign mode again. We used the media to broadcast our success stories of being parents, having careers, owning homes and so forth and explained how our PA service enabled us to live equal to nondisabled people. We won this battle, but soon after the Government decided to cut the mobility allowance. The attack on disabled people living in austerity was brutal. We couldn't get this decision reversed and people most in need do not have access to it.

In 2013 we set up the Clare Leader Forum, a disabled people's organisation. We focus on peer support, shared learning and human rights of all disabled people, and welcome people with all impairments. I've learned more in the last four years about inclusive activism than I have in all my years as an activist.

I often reflect on how we've achieved so much, and how much we struggle. We are expected to participate on one level and yet we are excluded on another. We need to explore the emotional dimension of our lived experiences as exclusion has its impact. I am grateful to have worked in the area of mental-health recovery as people in recovery have taught me what peer support is. In moving forward, we need to have empathy with each other. In addition, we need to be more inclusive of people with psychosocial, intellectual and sensory impairments, and remain open to learning from each other's experiences. Thank you for the journey so far.

Dermot Hayes

I was born in 1954, the same year as Martin Naughton, outside Corofin in north Clare. I was one of fourteen children. I came from a working-class background. It was common at the time for a lot of boys my age to drop out of school, but because of my disability, I stayed in school while my six brothers dropped out at Inter Cert level. I wasn't really built to get involved in sport, so instead I became involved with the local youth centre from the age of about fourteen or so. I took on leader-ship roles, and I was chairman, secretary and treasurer at various times. It became one of the most active youth clubs in the county during the seventies. Working in the youth club gave me great confidence in my ability to organise events.

When I was eighteen years old, I worked for a year and then I decided that manual work wasn't for me. In 1973 I raised some money and went to college in Cork to do electronics. By that Christmas, we'd found out that the whole school was a sham, that they'd taken our money but we were not going to get any qualification. From there, I started working in a company making electronic goods called Interton, and I was elected to be shop steward, a role I fulfilled for six years. I learned about injustice and inequality and the importance of standing up to people. At the time women weren't getting equal pay for doing the same job as men. The Equal Pay Act came in late 1976, and the fight for that was the first major campaign that I took part in. I became president of the local branch of the ITGWU trade union in Clare, then I became the chairman of the local Trade Council. I had the opportunity to speak at various conferences across the country on different issues, including rights for workers, participation and inclusion in the workplace, and equality for women. My factory closed down in 1983, which came as a big blow as many people, including myself, were dependent on the income.

In September 1983 I received a scholarship from the trade union to go back to college, to UCC in Cork, to study co-operative studies. For the first time, we had discussions about gay rights and inclusion of diverse communities, particularly immigrants. The course was designed to give people from different walks of life an opportunity to speak for themselves. The University ran a number of campaigns in the early eighties. FÁS courses were running at the time, under a different name. The quality of the training was poor and often the participants did not get jobs at the end of the scheme. We protested against that constantly.

When the cooperative studies course ended, I travelled around the country doing work placements. I met people from different backgrounds and became involved in the cooperative. I have great belief in the cooperative method of doing things. A friend of mine had set up a workers' cooperative in Corofin. It was made up of a crowd of radicals from our area who had worked in Dublin. Then we had others who arrived in Ireland from England who didn't agree with Maggie Thatcher and people from France who didn't agree with the French regime. I was involved in the cooperative for ten years and loved being exposed to the diverse opinions and lifestyles, and contributing to various discussions.

In 1992 we set up Disabled People of Clare, which included activists such as Ann Marie Flanagan, Jerome Finucane, Thomas Connole, Declan Considine, Tony Coogan, Geraldine Keane and others. Some of the main issues that we were facing included unemployment, lack of access, housing and low income. We worked well together, and it was a creative time. Martin Naughton came to visit us for the first of many times in 1993. We arranged a meeting at Spanish Point with Jana Overbo, a disabled woman who had come from the US to live in Ireland in the early nineties. We got to know Donal Toolan and Joe T. Mooney. We became involved with the Community Employment (CE) scheme and I became the CE Supervisor. By 1995, we were employing ten staff. Personal assistance and transport were our main focus. With the funding we received from the National Lottery in 1996, we bought a bus. We got to know all the councils and learned how the system worked. However, we were quite critical of the National Rehabilitation Board (NRB) locally in County Clare because their solution for finding jobs for people with disabilities was to put them into a training centre. We were adamant that we wanted real education, real training and real jobs. Other Centres for Independent Living (CILs) were being established around the country, and there was great vibrancy around Ireland at the time.

In 1997 we moved into the "big office" in Ennis

and we addressed the local county council and the urban council. We became good friends with the urban council clerk at the time; his mother was a wheelchair user herself, so he had a lot of empathy for us. One of the things we worked on together was accessible toilets for Ennis, and he got the funds together for two. We also got to address the local council chamber about access, and we were good at getting coverage in the local media.

Issues continued to arise, including the matter of personal assistance. We got on to the local Health Board, as it was then, and we sat on a committee that represented health and disability issues. We were lucky to have a couple of sympathetic ears that listened to us. In 1995 we set up a company with a board of directors. We were watching the Forum of People with Disabilities, which had a similar constitution, and we adapted their one for our organisation in Clare. We decided that the majority of our board had to be people with disabilities. I had been on the Forum of People with Disabilities and I found it quite progressive. There were quite tense meetings to do with various disabilities and actions.

The Disabled People of Clare was involved in many things. We got European funding for researching

entitlements for people with disabilities. We gathered all
the information relating to entitlements and put them on
a CD, the most accessible way to share information at the
time. We also got money from the Arts Council in 1997.
We had a chat locally with Peter Curtis, who has produced
more than sixty albums for various artists, and he wrote
a play called *Awaken the West*. We recruited a couple of
directors to help us perform the play. It was great to see disabled people in Clare executing this project. We brought
the play to Belfast and Dublin. It was a powerful way of
spreading the message of rights for people with disabilities.
We were always conscious of those all-important mantras:
"rights not charity" and "nothing about us without us" and
actively promoted them in the local media.

By 2002 the DPOC was employing around forty-
five people. I wanted a change and I started to look
around to see what was out there. Employability was
looking for a new manager, and I fancied the role. I got
the job, but after nine months of a probation period, the
boss pulled me aside and told me that she had decided
to let me go.

People with Disabilities in Ireland (PWDI) produced a major document in 1996, which was launched
down in Cork. The DPOC set up a local committee of

the PWDI in Clare. In 2003 I got a job with PWDI, which entailed going around the Munster area, supporting groups that were being set up in each county. Thanks to my extensive experience in the Independent Living Movement, I was able to help set up groups in Cork, Limerick, Tipperary, Kerry and Waterford.

Around this time the Disability Act was coming to fruition. The legislation that was proposed in 2002 wasn't written from a rights-based approach. In 2002 a group of us travelled to a meeting in the Mansion House in Dublin. The meeting was chaired by *Irish Times* journalist Fintan O'Toole. I spoke at length about why the proposed Disability Act was not sufficient. I felt it gave no rights to people with disabilities. The proposed act was scrapped. When the act was due to be passed in 2005, we again raised issues about people having no sign language, having no access to education, having no access to buildings, both public and private, and the accessibility of information. There was great hope that the Disability Act would deliver everything, but people had lost the guts to fight, and so the act was passed without mention of any rights. There were also many loopholes that allowed discrimination. A lot of people were disappointed with the Disability Act, but that's what we had to work with.

Part of my job was to encourage people to campaign for change. I travelled to Donegal, Sligo, Leitrim and Mayo. I was disappointed that bigger organisations such as the Irish Wheelchair Association didn't get involved with PWDI. It was also difficult to get people with disabilities involved because, as always, the lack of transport was a huge issue. We didn't have Zoom like we do today. I felt that we needed specific things to focus on. Transport and personal assistance were our biggest issues, as well as sign language and access to education. As time went on, education became easier for people with disabilities to access. You can see from the numbers how much the education system has changed in twenty years. A lot more people are participating now.

In 2009 PWDI were holding conferences around the country. However, there was never enough momentum to lead to a national movement. We had the resources but the leadership wasn't there. The whole set-up was too top-heavy; too many people on the board. Then the recession hit in 2008, and in 2011 the place closed down and I lost another job.

There are many issues that still need to be addressed. I think it's key to have the right to personal assistance.

Also, I think having access to housing is a huge issue, as people with disabilities, by and large, have Disability Allowance or social welfare as their only income. If people are to access decent accommodation, they need a proper system to support that. We also need to encourage the unification of people with disabilities. I look at the farmers, and I know that they were always united on their issues through the Irish Farmers' Association, and they made great progress. The trade union movement is being brought to bear on issues that concern us, like equality and participation. We have a great opportunity to do something significant for people with disabilities, and I know the trade unions have done a little, but collectively they could do more. We saw what could be done through the divorce campaign and with the marriage equality referendum campaign. We have to get away from the notion of charity. Even in my own county, people are caught between supporting the Clare Leader Forum and at the same time supporting the charity model here and elsewhere. You have to be clear where you draw the line.

I was nominated by Minister Kathleen Lynch in 2012 to the Disability Consultative Committee, which is a part of the National Disability Authority. We are still trying to roll out the Disability Act 2005, and we are sitting on various committees within different government departments. Progress is slow. For example, I'm on the housing committee, which is moving a little bit, but the problem with housing is that each county does its own thing to some degree. Other departments, including the Department of Transport, are also moving slowly. In Clare the public bus between Kilrush and Ennis is not accessible, and there are many other examples of such deficiencies across the country.

It was 2012 and the DPOC was still ticking on. Ann Marie Flanagan and I were still on the board, although I wasn't as active as when I had been involved with PWDI. Certain people on the board wanted to run a charity-model type thing, but we objected to that. When the manager left, we decided to scale back the job and the pay. We recruited somebody but she only lasted five days before resigning. We found a new person but she wanted the same salary as the previous manager. The DPOC eventually closed in 2016 due to financial difficulties.

Meanwhile I was appointed to the board of the Centre for Independent Living in 2015, which later became Independent Living Movement Ireland (ILMI). I served on the board for five years, stepping down in 2020. Thankfully ILMI is up and running, and I am proud of the great work that the board is doing. We've made great connections around the country, and it provides hope for a lot of people with disabilities. The most significant thing is that the Independent Living Movement now is thankfully stronger than it was twenty years ago. The idea that personal assistance should be legislated for is now embedded in our psyche.

Ireland is on the cusp of significant change, but unfortunately the charity model is still there. The big organisations are embedded in the charity model and jobs and livelihoods are dependent on it. As an independent living organisation, we must be clear that we want rights, not charity. To be included in society means to have access to services like everyone else. Technology can do so much in facilitating access to education and sign language. Those who are visually impaired can have full access to information. People can now be involved to whatever extent they feel comfortable with.

I stood for office on three occasions. The first time was back in 1985, when I sought election on behalf of the Workers' Party, which later morphed into Democratic Left. Ennis was a small town, and seventy-five votes could secure a seat on the Urban Council, but I only got seventy. In 2014 I stood again for the Labour Party, only to be pipped to the post once more. Then in 2019 I ran in the election as an independent. It was a tough campaign because my health wasn't great. I came eighth out of fifteen candidates. Although we had good coverage on social media, we were up against the big parties – Fianna Fáil and Fine Gael. I was covering the issues of homelessness, housing, disability and rights. To some degree I think we should have a system similar to the one in Australia where people have to vote or otherwise pay a fine, because only 60 per cent of Irish people vote.

The Clare Leader Forum has learned a lot from our mistakes. We have a broad church now, with people with all kinds of disabilities involved. It's more informal in structure than the DPOC was. We've learned how to cater for people's individual needs and how we can work together. We have a lot of common interests, whether it's our quarterly disco or transport issues. We were fortunate to get Limerick Institute of Technology on board as well; we've done three training courses with them so far. Technology has helped us in working together too, be it WhatsApp or Zoom. It gives us the space to question the charity model and compare it with the rights model. We've got more access now to the local authority, and through the Clare Public Participation Network we've had members voted onto local committees. It's our voice, and we are clear that it's "nothing about us without us". But there's a lot of work to be done yet, and discussions about the UN Convention and legislation comes up frequently. We also train people around advocacy, which is a huge issue for people with intellectual disabilities, and promote understanding of mental health issues. We have talented people who can do this within the disability movement in Clare and beyond.

We need to build a movement of disabled people who see independent living and human rights as a way forward. The charity model is not the solution. ILMI needs to watch what the government is doing and sit at the table to ensure that promises are delivered, including Personal Assistance Services. People should be able to make their own life choices.

Colm Whooley

I acquired my spinal injury in 1980 in a motorcycle accident on my way home from work. I was twenty-one, working in advertising as a graphic artist. I spent eight months in the National Rehabilitation Hospital (NRH). After my rehabilitation, I was still able to work because I worked at a desk. But I wasn't able to go back to the office, because it was in a Georgian building on Baggot Street and it wasn't accessible. I started to work freelance, but I felt isolated, so I went back to college to study architectural drafting and engineering. It wasn't just about what I was studying – I wanted to deal with the reality of my disability. I only briefly practised architecture or engineering, but it always helped me when it came to reviewing accessibility.

For the first ten years after the accident, campaigning and activism were not part of my life. After some time, I ended up back out in the NRH for a couple of months. This time it was different. The first time I was there, I was very much focused on me, but now I was seeing these "new" people with spinal-cord injuries. When I got talking to them, they had no expectations about returning to work. I would ask them what they were doing, and a significant number were just at home looking out the window. This, and an experience I had going for a job interview really got me thinking about getting more involved in disability issues.

The interview was with a disability organisation where I was interviewed by a panel of five people. None of them had a disability. At the end of it, they asked me if they could have improved the interview process, and I suggested it would have been nice as a disability organization if there had been a person with a disability on the panel. This really annoyed me, it was an organisation that was supposed to be a disability organisation, but I didn't see one person in the building with a disability.

From here, I thought about setting up an organisation. It was supposed to be short-term – I was focused on getting back to work – but I stayed involved with Spinal Injuries Ireland for more than twenty-one years. Back in the early nineties, there was a drive towards independent living. Disabled people were starting to have a voice. I had few links with people with disabilities because I'd just gone back into the mainstream. But I was hearing stuff on the radio, I was seeing it written about in the newspapers, and I said to myself, "That's what I'm talking about." One thing that struck me was that there were so many people speaking on our behalf. I would see these people speaking on the six o'clock news about people they were "helping" or "supporting". That bothered me.

One day my wife turned around to me and told me to go and do something about it. I approached the matron at the NRH because I had no contacts, and told her I was setting up an organisation. I was expecting her to say that it was a mad idea but instead she said, "Yep, go for it!" They gave us an office space in the hospital, and some names, and it started from there. Over the next twenty-one years, I became very involved and was fortunate to link up with people like Martin Naughton, John Doyle and lots of others. Martin and John touched a chord with me. When the protests around personal assistance started outside Leinster House in 1994, John Doyle befriended me and introduced me to people. John impressed me because for him it was all about the issues and what he could do for other people. Whenever I needed to be educated, I'd pick up the phone and say, "John, I'm hearing about these issues, can you fill me in?" John was a huge resource over those years, up until he passed away in 2017.

At the start of our journey at Spinal Injuries Ireland, we were so naïve, and we thought we could sort out a number of issues within twelve months. However, I realised that we were pushing against entrenched views. We reached out to people by creating a newsletter and a magazine and we were able to get access to people's details through the hospital. Because we were based in the hospital, we had a lot of interaction with the new patients. There were around 1,200 people with spinal injuries around the country, and so we thought, *Oh, this affects 1,200 people*. But then we realised that it doesn't just affect the individual; it also has a massive effect on the family. While we never claimed to bring clinical expertise, we offered peer support on what it was like to live with a disability.

From here, we set up a Community Employment (CE) scheme and we discovered that if someone was on Invalidity Pension, they weren't allowed to take part in CE schemes. We campaigned to get that changed and we were then able to take on people who were on Invalidity Pension, which was a great victory. We tried for years to ensure that the medical card was available to those who needed it and not tied to income. A huge volume of people entering employment and college were afraid of losing their medical cards, and this remains an issue.

I was involved in setting up an organisation in Europe called ESCIF, which was a spinal injuries organisation in Europe. I went to Switzerland, where they had vocational programmes in their rehabilitation centres. They thought it was madness to let people go home without enabling or supporting them in going back to work. When I saw the figures, the percentage of people with spinal injuries returning to work in Switzerland was up in the eighties, whereas Ireland was down in the twenties. The Swiss kindly translated their vocational programme into English for me, then we tweaked it and after a lot of discussion and amendments, we got the NRH to put a vocational programme in place. However, we have a long way to go. In my work coaching other disabled people, I've been saddened by their low expectations, not just on the part of the individual, but their parents too. I blame some of the organisations that are "supporting" them. We need to be creating expectations and resourcing people.

During my time at Spinal Injuries Ireland, a British charity asked me to go over to Nepal to give some guidance on setting up a similar organisation to Spinal Injuries Ireland there. I realised that hearing what was possible in Ireland gave them a reference point. I was there giving a talk, and before I started, a young girl who had sustained a spinal cord injury put up her hand and said, "I have two goals. I'm going to go to college and get a job." In general, expectations weren't huge because they didn't have the same resources we had back in Ireland. I mentioned that I was married, and afterwards that young girl came up to me and said, "I now have three goals. As well as college and finding work, I'm going to get married." The experience taught me the importance of role models and reference points. I still think there are disabled people out there who don't have the support or the resources to help them to become active members of their communities.

We need to look at how we can resource disabled people directly, and consider how we can support them in becoming active. I remember years ago when disabled people talked about working from home there was resistance, but we have to recognise that many disabled people live in rural areas, or that there may be other factors to be considered. The Covid-19 pandemic has changed attitudes. Working from home and using Zoom has become the norm for the whole community – not just for disabled people. This will create opportunities for disabled people in employment, and they will need to be supported. Zoom is a great way to reach the disabled person who's living in a very rural area or the person in the city who doesn't have transport or the PA hours. There are resources we have now that, if Martin Naughton or the others had access to in the nineties, there's no telling what they would have achieved! Social media also offers an opportunity to reach out to people.

We need to empower disabled people with a single voice. Until we do that, service providers will continue to speak on our behalf. I think we've regressed from where we were in the early nineties. We don't have the same presence. I remember when the budget would come out in the late nineties and there would be a whole section on disability issues. Now it's a little piece in the corner; we're an afterthought.

I remember one of the days John Doyle asked me to go into Government Buildings with Martin Naughton and a few others including activist Shelly Gaynor. Martin was well known, and the politicians were patting him on the shoulder and saying, "Oh, you're doing such great work." Politicians shouldn't patronise us; they should take us seriously and support our agenda. In the 1990s we took to the streets about PA services, and there were changes. But we seem to have lost that collective passion, it is very much more fragmented. We need a shared, one-voiced message with clear demands, under one banner.

Disabled people have lost ground and the disability industry has become stronger and more vocal. I can't remember the last time an organisation (apart from ILMI, of course) asked me what issues affect me. I don't blame these organisations. I blame us, the disability community. We need to take control back. If we don't, we're just going to become a commodity generating an income for an ever-growing disability industry. If we don't continue to raise our voice, we may not retain the breakthroughs in PA services and other changes brought about by disability activists in the 90s.

Talking from the perspective of a coach who coaches both disabled and non-disabled people, coaching is about challenging people to think. I know a term that isn't always appreciated by the disability community is "people who inspire people", but John Doyle inspired me. Martin Naughton inspired me. The community has a history and we need to let the next generation know what has been achieved, and support them to continue to move things forward. When I think back to when I had my accident, the general public's attitude to disabled people was in the Dark Ages compared to where we are now. We need to create a platform for disabled people to ask questions, both of themselves and of others. When I had my accident, a nun gave me a book from America – she'd been over there – about people in the US with spinal injuries who'd done amazing things. I always remember one particular guy in it who'd gone kayaking, and his level of injury was higher than mine, and I remember thinking, *If he can do it, why can't I do it?* Years later, I took up kayaking simply because of that piece in that book. Again, this shows the value of reference points and role models.

We all know the vocal disabled people out there who are very confident; we've seen them on TV and heard them on the radio and indeed on the ILMI podcasts, but they are the exception rather than the rule, and we need to encourage activists to become more vocal. If ILMI becomes the place where people feel part of the movement, this will give us a huge voice and also give people a sense that they're part of something. We can no longer depend on individuals like Martin, Eugene and John. If it becomes about individuals, we're losing. We need to focus on specific issues and campaigns to drive us forward. If we want the government to change things, we need to let them know that we mean business. We need people to recognise that we are a large part of our community. In short, we need a forum, a voice and an agenda, and we need to resource disabled people to move that forward.

Michael McCabe

I was born with cerebral palsy, with a significant disability. Like a lot of my counterparts, I went to a special school, where the staff had no expectations for people like me. They tried to educate me as best they could. It's funny that thirty years or more later, three of my counterparts from that special school ended up founding the Centre for Independent Living, with three other people.

I left school at eighteen, with little in the way of reading and writing skills. My doctor got me into the Central Remedial Clinic (CRC), and this woke me up and made me realise that I had no education. They helped me with my language, my vocabulary and my reading. So that's where I started.

My first memory of advocacy was in the CRC. There was a long corridor, broken up by a number of sliding doors at intervals. A young girl there who was about three or four years old took a shine to me. One day she was wearing callipers on her legs and they got caught in the grooves of the sliding door. Everyone was just walking by her, so I went and got the physiotherapist. That's my first memory of advocacy. I was about twenty-three, twenty-four at the time. Of course, I didn't know that it was advocacy then. The physiotherapist nominated me for an award at the CRC for doing that.

I was sixteen when I joined the Irish Wheelchair Association (IWA). There was a club on Thursday nights. The chap who organised it, Paddy Crookes, had muscular dystrophy and he lived very near me in Cabra. He came round and we used to go out to cabaret clubs. He was a bit of a singer – he used to enter competitions. One night he asked me to go out, but there was a problem – we had a lift going out but we had no way to get home. We went with my sister to The Talk of the Town, a cabaret club over on the southside of Dublin. At the end of the night, we were sitting outside the building and we didn't know what we were going to do. A few of the lads who were passing by asked us if we were all right. I explained that we had no way of getting home. One of them said, "I have a van around the corner, I'll be back in a minute." There were four powerchairs in all, and they just lifted us into their van and brought us home! This made me a lot more confident in myself. Unfortunately, Paddy passed away a few years later.

All through my life I've been building on my own confidence. My parents, especially my mother, had a lot to do with this; I was always treated the same as everyone else. I did some development courses with the IWA, and I got very involved in the branches and worked my way up until I was elected to the board and then became chairperson for nine years. I met many people. Liam Maguire was a person who I admired. I was the first person with a speech impairment to achieve what I achieved.

Then of course I met Martin Naughton. I don't know whether that was my downfall, but the social workers and the occupational therapists got a group together. Myself, Martin and about nine others were in that group and the Centre for Independent Living grew from there. I was Chairperson of IWA at that time, around 1991, so through the association I was able to get the loan of a bus, and a group of us travelled to the UK to learn about independent living.

I suppose I should share a few of the funny things. A friend of mine was driving the bus, but we had to get somebody else to come with me as a support; this was before personal assistants. I didn't know anybody, so I got a young man to help me. The first night we got to the hotel, when we got to the bedroom, there was only one bed. I normally sleep in my "birthday suit" (in other words, I normally wear nothing). It was a bit awkward. The next morning, my friend Morgan, the driver, knew there was something wrong. I told him what had happened and he said, "Did you not know that there's a bed that you can pull out from under the bed?" Needless to say, I was a bit compromised! Martin was very shrewd. We would get up early in the morning, drive for five hours, have a meeting, and drive for another two hours to where we were staying. But they were all hotels with no bars. We had planned to be up half the night! We were awake for about four days and it was hard going. You really had to concentrate at those meetings, but we still had fun, too.

I met many people with disabilities at all different levels. Some had PAs, while others were working on other projects, but they were all under the philosophy of independent living. When we came back home, we set up a Centre for Independent Living (CIL). I was in the background a lot of the time because of my other position at the IWA. I had a number of jobs. I started off as a training officer.

Martin asked me to make up a programme for leaders and PAs. None of us had any experience bar Martin, who was a businessman. The first thing I did was get a bit of paper and mark off coffee breaks, lunch and afternoon breaks. Martin asked me if he could have a look, so that didn't go down well! But we got there. Then he asked me to be an operations manager. So I had to come up with ideas and new ways of doing things. In 1994 a CIL opened in Blanchardstown, and I was manager there. I was also on the management committee in Carmichael House. I did a lot of the day-to-day management in Carmichael.

I cannot remember whether it was the first or the second demonstration we had outside the Dáil – I was working with Audrey Brodigan inside with the government trying to do a deal. Martin was the only one there. We were able to get in through two of Bertie Ahern's advisors, and we did a deal that took us off the street. After that, Martin stopped the demonstration.

We were breaking new ground, but at the time we didn't realise how radical it was. There were people before us but I think we brought it to another level. Unfortunately, I don't think younger people realise you have to do more than just talk, and I think they need to put their bodies where their mouths are. I don't mean this to reflect badly on anyone.

Some of our peers were Hubert McCormack, the late Ursula Hegarty, Peter Moore, the late Declan O'Keefe and the late Dermot Walsh. I have to admit that everything wasn't always rosy. Sometimes you have to be a diplomat. There was one incident when Martin and I had a difference of opinion. One Saturday he came around to my house, and we had a hell of a row, and my wife, Sinéad, got upset, so I told him to get out. He did apologise after, though. That was the one thing about Martin and me – we'd have a row but if we needed anything, we would lift the phone.

The CILs in Blanchardstown and Dublin 7 started one after the other, and then we expanded throughout the country. The main ones are still there, like Clare, Cork, Donegal and Offaly, where you have one or two strong members. They seemed to last the best. In the early days, my other job was interviewing people like Joe T. Mooney. I went up to Donegal to interview him when he was hiring his PA. Then I went down to Michael Nestor in Offaly and interviewed him in the garden. That was another part of my gig that I enjoyed – helping people to understand the philosophy of independent living. Sometimes it can be difficult to help people truly understand it.

The philosophy is very difficult to put into words. It's more of a state of mind. You have to believe that your disability doesn't matter, and although people are helping you to do what you can't do, you're not *relying* on them.

In terms of the start of Independent Living, we were only looking at the present. We weren't looking down the road to see what was ahead, because what if you do that and it doesn't work? You have to believe that what you're doing is going to make a difference, and not think about next year or the year after. We also need to look at the wider European picture. Martin was very good because he and John Evans in the UK started up the European Network for Independent Living (ENIL). I don't know if many people know that for a number of years the secretariat for ENIL was in Ireland. John Dolan was on the board as well, not known to me of course. I think the people coming forward now need to look further than Ireland, and that's why the freedom drive is very important. We need to allow things to come from the top down – from Europe – because it's harder to do it from the bottom up. I know we are making more progress with the European convention, but that's going to take a long time to truly take hold.

In one particular act of protest, which was outside the offices of the European Parliament in Dublin, Martin and I dressed in matching black and white prison uniforms. It was done on the spur of the moment. Nina Byrne built a cage for us. I was very surprised because Martin didn't normally do things like that. We protested for about four hours and people were stopping and offering us money, and we had to tell them that it wasn't about money. I have the photo on my laptop as a screensaver. It was just the two of us in a "prison cell" – you can't see the wheelchairs, just the two of us. We were doing it in the hope that Europe would do more about personal assistance and let people live their lives and not be prisoners in their own homes. It was also about ratifying the UNCRPD.

I have spoken in the European Parliament. I've chaired a meeting with the Irish MEPs, which wasn't easy because Martin was shouting in the background all the time. He was speaking over everyone, of course, while I was trying to keep some sort of order!

I'm very happy that there seem to be so many highly focused people involved in ILMI. People like me, we don't last – a lot of good people have passed away. A few years ago, I was worried about the way things were going because we were trying to get people involved who didn't want to be. I think the future is good, and I think we need to get more vocal and make ILMI's job easier!

Sarah Fitzgerald

It was June 2005 and I was twenty-one years old. I was studying at Trinity College, one of the most prestigious colleges in the world. I was completely self-sufficient, living in Dublin and supporting myself financially. I thought that I knew everything, having that smug arrogance that young people usually have. Alas, I was looking for something – a summer job. My personal assistant at the time, Mary, told me that she'd been given a contact for a man who could apparently find me a job. *Doing what?* I wondered. People don't just get handed jobs, not in the real world anyway, and I refused any tokenistic gestures. How did a man who I'd never met before in my life have a job for me?

I remember putting on my cheap Dunnes suit, the one I kept for job interviews, and going with Mary to Chief O'Neill's in Smithfield to meet this man. Mary told me his name was Martin Naughton. That name meant nothing to me; I'd never heard of him before. Apparently, Mary said, he was high up in the disability sector or something like that. I had no idea that I was on my way to meet one of the founders of the Independent Living Movement in Ireland. So there I was, waiting in Chief O'Neill's, when a man in a red jumper and matching red hat whizzed into the room. Martin was not how I'd imagined him at all. Honestly, I hadn't expected him to be a wheelchair user. This moment marked the beginning of me challenging my own negative internalised beliefs. He oozed charisma, charm and authority all at once. I didn't know whether to be mesmerised or terrified.

"Do you know what a leader forum is?" he asked me.

I said of course I did. Who didn't? He smiled and told me that no one did, that it was a new concept devised by Eugene Callan to create a strong collective of leaders who would represent themselves. He then told me that I was going to establish a leader forum in Dublin, and not to let him down. I took the responsibility seriously.

When I returned home, I took out my laptop and did what I should've done before the interview: I googled Martin Naughton. Not much came up – some basic information about how he started the Independent Living Movement, but nothing particularly exciting. However, when I started going to Carmichael House for work, some pieces started falling into place. I met Donal Toolan, who told me many little anecdotes about himself and Martin. Through establishing the leader forum, I also met Eileen Daly and Maureen McGovern, both of whom share their experiences in this collection.

Three years later, I found myself working for Offaly Centre for Independent Living as a researcher. Again, it struck me how little information was available about the movement in Ireland. I knew from reading about Ed Roberts and the establishment of the first Center for Independent Living, in Berkeley, California, that Independent Living was the product not of medical need but political activism. I listened to, watched and read interviews with Ed Roberts and Judy Heumann. But something was still missing for me. Where were the Irish stories? I knew – because I had been told – that the first Irish Centre for Independent Living was established in Carmichael House in 1992. But who was involved? What drove them to bring about change? Little did I know that in the early nineties, activists such as Jacqui Browne and Peter Kearns, along with the late Donal

Toolan and others, had been instrumental in establishing the Commission on the Status of People with Disabilities, which published its revolutionary report in 1996. This marked a move towards disabled people in Ireland being seen as citizens deserving of rights, a move away from being treated as objects of care.

I developed an insatiable hunger for the personal stories of disabled activists. I wanted to know what work they had done, what they had sacrificed to ensure that privileged disabled people like me were not automatically sent to the local special school. I wished to know more about the generation who fought to ensure that my life was a little easier than theirs. In my role at Offaly Centre for Independent Living, I compiled a short collection of stories by leaders and personal assistants. But it wasn't enough. I was greedy. I wanted more.

It wasn't until 2016 that an opportunity arose in the most unorthodox way. It was 13 October, soon to be remembered as an unlucky day indeed. There were awful rumours circulating on social media that Martin Naughton had passed away. I was in denial. It wasn't possible. I didn't believe it until I saw the official RTÉ report. I cried, as I know many others did. A week later I was sitting in Carmichael House with a group of activists, trying to decide how to honour Martin's memory. I felt like an imposter and yet felt at home all at once. I remember silently looking at the photos on the walls of that little office, photos of Martin, of Donal and of other great activists, and wondering what part I could play in collecting the history of a movement that was by then changing the trajectory of my entire future.

By Us With Us, a memorial event for our fallen peers, took place in September 2017. Never before have I felt such a strong sense of solidarity and belonging. My favourite part of the entire project was talking to people and listening to their stories. Some memories were bittersweet, others were hilarious but far too outrageous for the public domain. I started to truly understand the importance of camaraderie and friendship within a social movement, and how acknowledging and respecting different opinions and viewpoints is key to building a collective.

It is only in my adult life that I have started to take a real interest in history, and I think I know why. For many, history is about remembering dates and locations, and often it involves reading about people we have no personal connection to. That was the case with me too, at least until Martin's passing. Now, through hearing stories of Martin and other activists, I can appreciate why many disabled people, including the ones who share their stories in this collection, dedicated their time to promoting equality for all of us. Some of the storytellers in this collection still wrestle with the shackles of internalised oppression, having fought for years to fit in. Through these stories, the psychological damage of trying to feel "normal" through physio and other therapies is evident. For some, the experience of institutionalisation was scarring and isolating, while for others it enabled them to develop confidence and to find allies among their peers. Others were not comfortable with identifying as disabled until they themselves saw the positivity and strength contained within the label itself. This diversity is a vital component in the disability movement. It is a reminder to others – and to ourselves – that although we can come together as a collective to create change, disabled people are not a homogeneous group, but rather we are individuals with our own opinions and perspectives.